D0112091

LIBERATING THE LAITY

EQUIPPING ALL THE SAINTS FOR MINISTRY

R. PAUL STEVENS

Foreword by Carl Armerding

INTERVARSITY PRESS
DOWNERS GROVE, ILLINOIS 60515

InterVarsity Press is the book-publishing division of Inter-Varsity Christian Fellowship, a student movement active on campus at hundreds of universities, colleges and schools of nursing. For information about local and regional activities, write IVCF, 233 Langdon St., Madison, WI 53703.

Distributed in Canada through InterVarsity Press, 860 Denison St., Unit 3, Markham, Ontario L3R 4H1, Canada.

The cartoons in this book first appeared in Leadership, a CTi publication, and are used by permission.

All quotations from Scripture are from the Holy Bible, New International Version. Copyright © 1973, 1978, International Bible Society. Used by permission of Zondervan Bible Publishers.

Cover illustration: Roberta Polfus

ISBN 0-87784-613-8

Printed in the United States of America

Library of Congress Cataloging in Publication Data
Stevens, R. Paul, 1937-

   Liberating the laity.

   Includes bibliographical references.
   1. Laity.   2. Lay ministry.   I. Title.
BV4400.S715   1985   253   85-10856
ISBN 0-87784-613-8

17	16	15	14	13	12	11	10	9	8	7	6	5	4	3	2	1
99	98	97	96	95	94	93	92	91	90	89	88	87	86	85		

*Dedicated
to
my father and mother
who were the first
to equip me
for
this life
and
the next*

Foreword

Paul Stevens graduated from seminary with some radical ideas. Despite the traditional roles of clergy and laity assumed in his theological training, he kept finding in New Testament Christianity a much different model of the church. In place of hierarchy (worse yet, democracy), he observed theocracy (a body with God in Christ as its only head); leadership was provided through "elders among the people" *(laos)*, equipping and encouraging the ministry gifts given to the whole church by the Holy Spirit. Some of these elders were supported in full-time ministry, but they were always plural; they never constituted a separate class from the laity, and most of them earned their living by secular employment.

A series of very successful pastorates failed to rid Paul of his dis-ease with the expectations placed on his role, by fellow clergy and laity alike. Despite attempts to reform the thinking of his lay members and with a growing chorus of New Testament scholarship affirming his position, Paul concluded that nothing short of a radical vocational step of faith was needed to make the point. That is where this book was born.

The evangelical and ecclesiastical communities were shocked. A leading practitioner of "professional" ministry in the city had resigned his pastorate—not to take a bigger charge or even to pursue writing and reflection, but to take up carpentry! Paul attached himself to a local businessman and painfully learned new skills in woodworking. For five years he earned his bread as any other elder, all the while continuing to give ministry leadership to a growing body of believers. It is no exaggeration to say that most of his colleagues thought he had gone a bit soft, while among the laity there was a tendency to wonder what unknown failure had caused him to "leave the ministry." A couple of key pastorates became open, for which Paul would otherwise have been a candidate, but no one was interested in a "former minister" who had broken ranks to be a carpenter. But God was blessing, and the lessons of this book were being forged in the crucible of a training Paul and Gail Stevens would never have received in school or the manse.

Yes, the decision was costly, the more so because Paul enjoyed the pastorate and was very good at it. But such powerful insights are not born in theoretical discussion; they must be worked out in life. If, as Whitehead observed, the average professional graduate is "overladen with inert ideas" and underequipped with practical applications, no one can charge Paul or his book with being average.

As one who has for five years worked as a fellow elder with Paul and as principal of Regent College, where Paul is teaching his concepts in a nontraditional theological setting, I am pleased to command both book and author. Not that Paul Stevens wants or needs commendation from me; his surpassing desire is to be found worthy by the One who shall judge rightly at the last day. And his book will commend itself. It takes what many New Testament scholars are convinced of, that the very concept of "clergy and laity" is absent from the pages of the New Testament, and fleshes out the theory in the context of a working body of Christians.

Paul Stevens's goal is clear: the abolition of the laity altogether. All the people of God—both so-called clergy and so-called laity—must be elevated to their true dignity as ministers of Jesus Christ. Here is no narrow anticlericism; this is rather the liberation of all the people of God! My advice is simple: read and heed, and pray that God will open the windows of heaven to bring about a revolution of the church in our day, one that will finally mobilize the whole people of God to do "the work of the ministry" (Eph 4:12 KJV).

Carl Edwin Armerding, B.D., Ph.D.
Principal, Regent College
Vancouver, British Columbia, Canada

Preface

This book is as accidental as my discovery of lay ministry. Had my colleague, George Mallone, not invited me to write with him a volume on equipping the laity for ministry, I would not have thought of *writing* about it since I am so enthusiastic about *doing* it. As it turned out, I wrote the whole book, for illness forced George to turn the balance of the project over to me. This second accident is an unhappy loss to the reader, for George is always looking for where the wave of renewal in the church is breaking, while I feel more comfortable in the gentle rollers that follow. But we share a common desire to see the renewal movement come of age through the complete equipping of the saints for the work of the ministry.

I stumbled across the idea of preparing all the saints for ministry during my seminary days. It was not in the curriculum. It was a benign accident. That the so-called pastor or minister is called not primarily to *do* the work of the ministry but to *equip* the saints for the ministry leaped off the pages of the fourth chapter of Paul's letter to the Ephesians. I have been possessed by that idea and the glory of it for twenty-five years. I am convinced that the liberation of the laity is not merely marginalia of New Testament Christianity but one of its central themes. And the purpose of liberating or equipping all the saints for ministry is not so that the load on pastors' shoulders will be eased through delegation of *their* ministry. Each believer needs to be equipped for *his* or *her own* ministry in the church and in the world.

This does not mean the demotion of the pastor and the promotion of the so-called layperson. For through equipping, both pastor and layperson are restored to their proper dignity. Elton Trueblood once wrote that "the idea of the pastor as the equipper is one which is full of promise, bringing back self-respect to men in the ministry when they are sorely discouraged by the conventional pattern. Here is a job that is as intrinsically hard, as the job of the official prayer at banquets is intrinsically easy. To watch for underdeveloped powers, to draw them out, to bring potency to actuality in human lives—this is a self-validating task."[1]

It is my hope that the book will be read by pastors *and* laypeople. Both need to be challenged and changed on this matter—*together.* This gracious conspiracy to bring about the full employment of the people of God is only gently hinted at in this book. Adequate treatment of the new style of pastoral leadership required for a full equipping ministry must await another volume.

For the present, I offer this volume as a humble attempt to move the heart of the church with the beauty and freedom of God's grand plan for his people. If I err on the side of passion and wear my heart on my sleeve at times, forgive me. It is not a day for one more program in lay training. It is a day for radical transformation of the whole people of God into a ministering people. Nothing short of that will restore the church to its pioneering role in the kingdom of God. May this consideration of equipping the laity for ministry be as fruitful to the reader as the living and writing of it has been to me.

As my wife Gail, my three children and my son-in-law well know, but for their constant encouragement I would not have completed this task. My mother-in-law, Irma Boulter, proofread the manuscript with exceptional care. Special thanks are due to my brothers and sisters in God's family who, over the years, have endured my attempts to live this book. Their encouragement—and sometimes their forgiveness—are major sources of inspiration.

Part I
Points of Departure: Experiential and Biblical

1. The Confessions of a Late-Starting Layperson

What's a pastor doing hammering nails?" A board member of my church asked me that question as she watched from her kitchen window. Raising her eyes from the sink, she spotted me, nail belt slung from my hips, working as a carpenter on a nearby home. It was part of my five-year plunge into the so-called lay ministry.

I was at that time the pastor of a large and thriving evangelical church. I loved my people and was loved by them. But my own teaching had caught up to me, and I was actually *doing* something about it. The hardest part of the Great Commission is not to go and make disciples of all nations, not even to teach them, but to teach them *to obey* (Mt 28:19-20). After twenty-five years of teaching the Bible as a pastor-teacher, what gripped my conscience were the areas that I had not yet applied to myself. One such area was that I had never supported myself in ministry by the work of my own hands or mind.

An Explosive Idea

In seminary I had accidentally picked up an explosive idea that was not in the curriculum of the college and is still scandalously missing as a training theme for seminarians. In my study of Ephesians 4, I discovered that the primary purpose of church leadership—leading ministers, pastor-teachers—was to "equip the saints for the work of the ministry."

In certain older translations of Ephesians 4:12 a fatal comma had been introduced which made it *seem* that the work of the pastor-teacher was *to do the work of the ministry* rather than to equip *all the saints* to do this work. According to this translation, God gave "apostles, some prophets, some evangelists, some pastors and teachers, for the equipment of the saints, [that's the fatal comma] for the work of ministry."[1] Thus it is not the saints but the leading equippers who do the ministry. However, there should be no comma between the last two phrases. More recent translations have corrected this error: God gave apostles, prophets, evangelists, pastors and teachers "for the equipment of the saints for the work of ministry."

But the equipping of the saints for ministry rests on a more certain biblical and theological foundation than the omission of a comma. It has a broad scriptural base, which this book will explore in theory and practice. It rests on the idea that the church—the whole church—is a priestly people. The New Covenant has made the weakest, most inadequate people competent to minister (2 Cor 3:4-6). God has poured out his power on the whole church in this Pentecostal age. It is a tragic spiritual anachronism that the contemporary church often seems like a house wired for electricity with the mains shut off. The church is a servant people, a kingdom people, a gifted people endowed with multifaceted gifts and graces of ministry.

Therefore it is the primary task of church leaders as well as the concern of every member that all the saints be equipped for their ministry. That is why I hope this book is read by pastors and laypeople together. Each must assist the other to make this possible. A whole new identity and priority for ministry must be found for both pastors and laypeople.

No one person could ever embody all the gifts for ministry given by God to the church. And no single person in the church can be the omnicompetent equipper of the laity. Bringing the laity into full liberation is a shared task.

The Ordination of a Reluctant Controversialist

While being examined by the ordination council in my first church in Montreal, Quebec, I made a statement which divided the council between the laity and clergy. I shared with them my view of ministry. I had a call to be an equipper. I was called to teach and preach God's Word. But I was not called to be a separated minister. I was no different from any other Christian who had taken the trouble to listen to God's call in his heart. While I would consider it a great privilege—and I still do—to be supported by the Lord's people in order to give concentrated attention to my ministry, I did not feel that it was essential that I be supported.

I was being examined for ordination by representatives of some twenty Baptist churches in the province. I treasure that day, not merely for myself but for every servant of God who has an enduring sense of call. But I keep the official record of it, my ordinational certificate, over my desk partly to remind me of what I am not. I am not the only ordained or commissioned minister of my church. I am not the only called person. I am not the only person who should be called a minister. If the institution of ordination perpetuates a practical heresy in the church by slighting the nonprofessional minister and favoring the professional, then it should be abolished. In a fine historical, exegetical and theological study of the practice of ordination, Vancouver scholar Marjorie Warkentin concluded that "the vocabulary of New Testament leadership permits no pyramidal forms, it is the language of horizontal relationships. . . . Ordination can have no function in such a system, for it sets up barriers where none should exist, that is, between one Christian and another and hinders the mutual service by which the church is edified."[2] I think there *is* a place for ordination. But if we are convinced that ministers that are fully supported by the church should be commissioned, then we must find some way to ordain the lay ministry also.

At my ordination examination, I made a prediction that for part of my life I might be supported by the Lord's people and for part of my life I may choose to, or may need to, support myself. I believed (and still believe) that I have a call to ministry but no call to the professional ministry. I do not believe there is a call directly from God to enter the professional ministry. The call to be supported comes largely from the Lord's people. Even then it requires discernment as to whether being supported would "hinder" the advancement of the gospel, as Paul intimated in his own case (1 Cor 9:12). When a person is called into a specific ministry and there is no initiative of support from the body, he or she is neither to go around begging for support nor to wait and pray. Scripture clearly gives a mandate to go out and to work.[3]

I am a reluctant controversialist sometimes caught between the intensity of my own convictions drawn from Scripture and my compelling desire to be liked and appreciated. So I found it hard to leave the room to let the ordination council pass judgment on my soul. What I suspected would happen, did. The laity were thrilled to be affirmed by an equal as an equal. The clergy were either threatened by a nonconforming neophyte or were genuinely concerned that something was lacking in my experience of the call of God. I was ordained anyway.

The examination was a terrifying trial. I felt as Luther must have felt at the Diet of Worms. The service of ordination followed immediately with the laying on of hands. I had a sense of being filled and cloaked with the Holy Spirit. Afterward I was permitted to use the title *reverend,* a term I have since tried unsuccessfully to avoid.

Over the twenty-four years that followed, I have had many opportunities to explore the idea of shared ministry. At Temple Baptist Church we formed a group ministry composed of the nonprofessional deacon-elders and myself. (One of them who became an outstanding model of the voluntary clergy—a "tentmaker"—will be introduced in chapter eleven.) But the transformation in this inner-city church was not as great as the transformation in my own soul.

The Earthing of Idealism
My youthful idealism of being separated for "prayer and the ministry of the Word" (Acts 6:4) needed to interact with the necessity of keeping

the church going, churning out the bulletin on the copier, keeping the flock well cataloged and starting the old coal-fired baptistry heater in the basement. As a young frustrated pastor, I soon grew weary of oiling every squeaky wheel and tracking down every disgruntled member. Once, over coffee with one of the deacons, I confessed that I was going to quit.

"Why?" he asked.

I sighed, "I feel like a firefighter. I hear about some growing fire of discontent and go there to put it out, only to hear of another one somewhere else. I'm tired of putting out fires."

This dear brother replied, "But you're the best damn firefighter we ever had!" It was a delightful backhanded compliment. And it helped me to explore a more strategic use of my time—equipping.

There at Temple Baptist Church I cut my teeth on the various realities of equipping that are developed in this book. Structure, I discovered, is important; there is no point in saying that every member is a minister if the structures of the fellowship "say" the exact opposite—by making it hard for people to discover their gifts or to exercise loving service. I had to put Ephesians 4:12 in context. (We will attempt this in chapter two, by exploring what kind of environment actually encourages ministry development.) I struggled with some of the leadership issues experienced by an equipper. If my role is to facilitate everyone else's ministry, will I have anything definite for myself? Little did I know that a call to deeper spirituality was implicit in the work of equipping, as I will share in chapter ten.

The principles I had drawn from Ephesians 4:12 were further unearthed and my vision for an equipping ministry widened when my wife Gail became a liberated layperson. She had always had a fruitful person-to-person ministry, not only at home with us, but with neighbors and church people as well. But this time she took what seemed to be a quantum leap forward. I felt that I was becoming a minister's husband! She was the first in our family to become involved in neighborhood evangelistic Bible studies, which were enormously fruitful. Then she plunged into inner-healing ministry. When she first went to a weekend conference where the diet was frankly "charismatic," I was cautious. A

*"We see our pastor as one who primarily administrates, enables, coordinates . . .
and scrapes the pigeon droppings off the steeple."*

friend of mine said, "She'll come back speaking in tongues, for sure."
This did not help me in the least.

There were no tongues when she came home but there was a fresh
vision of what God could do through visualized prayer: how God desires to heal the souls of people scarred by deep hurts and traumatic
family experiences. Gail was *accidentally* drawn into the leadership
group for the weekend and got pushed beyond her comfort zone into
new territory. She found herself praying for the kind of needy and hurting
people she had tried to help by conventional Christian counseling, but
now she saw God bring about substantial healing. Through that leadership accident, Gail was partially equipped for a new ministry. And I
learned something about facilitating "the equipment of the saints." They
need to be exposed to something more. They need opportunity to try

out various ministries, even prophecy and prayers for healing.

If only I could create in a local church the kind of leadership accident that gave Gail an opportunity to move forward. To be equipped, people need to take risks in a safe environment. One ideal place to do this is in a small group meeting in homes. I have great respect for Gail as a wife, a mother and a prayer-counselor. But I am most grateful that God has used her peculiar pilgrimage in ministry to help me reformulate some important principles for helping people grow and develop in the use of spiritual gifts.

About that time, God began to put his finger on both of us as we prayed about the possibility of starting a new church in a needy part of Vancouver. There were five founding members—that's about the same number Paul started with in Philippi. There was no possibility of being financially supported by the other four and, what is more important, I had an unpaid "bill" to pay to my own teaching. Until then I had not supported myself in what is wrongly called "secular" employment. A stint in the work world could be good for me. But I didn't even have a marketable skill.

The Anatomy of a Hard Decision

This was not the hardest decision of my life. We were so clearly led by God that we did not see how radical and costly the decision would be. What was hard was not making the decision but being content with it. There were colleagues in my denomination who warned me that I would be committing vocational suicide if I left a thriving work to become what Priscilla and Aquila were in Corinth and Ephesus: Tentmakers (Acts 18:1-3). I had no ambitions to climb the ecclesiastical ladder. But neither did I want to step off it without having the opportunity of getting on again. There were a few notable worthies who wondered about our mental health. I was also concerned about the effect of our move on the church we were presently serving and the degree to which this call could be shared by them—especially since we were committed to starting an interdenominational community church. I sought as much advice as I could get. But I needed confirmation from the Lord that this was truly his will and within his great purpose.

It has been my repeated experience that God equips the saints *through people* and sometimes through the most surprising people in the fellowship. Perhaps Paul had something like this in mind when he said that "those parts of the body that seem to be weaker are indispensable" (1 Cor 12:22). A young postgraduate student from India had come to the Lord through our ministry and I had discipled him in the Word for many months. But now it was his turn to disciple me. When we were on the verge of our decision, he stayed up all night in deep intercessory prayer on our behalf. God gave him three messages which he gave to us when we woke from our sleep. I now understand that these words were prophecy in the true New Testament sense of an inspired word from God for "strengthening, encouragement and comfort" (1 Cor 14:3). These were the words he gave:

"First, you are free to leave your present church.

"Second, you must not worry about that church; Jesus is the Head.

"Third, tentmaking will be a thorn in your flesh."

The third word, referring to Paul's continuing problem (2 Cor 12:7), was disturbing. I did not take this to mean that God was telling me not to support myself in ministry. Rather, I understood that God was gently warning me that it would not be as easy as I hoped, and it might not be easy to leave tentmaking when I might want to. The apostle himself had received at least one negative prophecy which was not a stop sign but a gracious warning by the Lord to count the cost (Acts 21:10-14).

A Christian brother graciously offered me a job as a carpenter. I had some natural affinity with this trade and more self-confidence than I should have had. Much of it disappeared the very day my former board member looked out her window and was amazed to see her pastor as a tradesman. I came home that night realizing that it would be a thorn. I was an apprentice carpenter at thirty-seven, afraid of heights and struggling not to swear when I hit my thumb instead of the nail. But this plunge into the lay world was for me the only way I could gain the experiential base for a larger equipping ministry.

Always a Layperson
I had never stopped being a layperson, biblically speaking, even when

I was a supported pastor. In the Bible, the laity (Greek, *laikoi*) is the whole people of God—both clergy and so-called laity. It is a term of honor since the whole people of God in Christ is chosen to be a "royal priesthood, a holy nation, a people *[laikoi]* belonging to God" (1 Pet 2:9). Christianity arose as an essentially lay movement and it was a long time before "lay" became a term for second-class status. Some pressure came from popular piety which used Old Testament models of priestly leadership and projected them into the church—even though in Christ the priestly privileges were extended to the whole church. In addition, with a growing sacramentalism, people demanded that a special person—the priest—dispense the sacraments, while the laity, the "populus," were the passive recipients.[4]

But the most pernicious influence in the decline of the laity is still with us: secularization by copying the world's leadership patterns. In the Greco-Roman world the municipal administration had two parts: the *klēros* (clergy), the magistrate and the *laos* (layperson), the ignorant and uneducated citizen. The same defamatory distinction prevails today when people argue for secular management structures in church organization and when, in response to an appeal for the full liberation of the laity, one hears the jibe, "Would you go for medical help to an untrained doctor? Why would you trust your soul to a nonprofessional?"

Several months had passed since I began my carpentry experience. Vancouver's drenching winter rain had turned our building site into a muck hole. The romance of being a carpenter for Christ—someone called me The Hallelujah Handyman—was fading. I felt the thorn. Standing there with mud up to the top of my gum boots—and sometimes over—I asked, "Now what exactly am I learning about the plight of the laity?"

I was learning that there are two kinds of lay ministry, one in the church and one in the world. Mark Gibbs and T. Ralph Morton categorize these as type A and type B. Laypersons of type A are interested primarily in a craft, a career or a profession, including the vocation of homemaking. Their focus for ministry is the church in dispersion, *diaspora*.

Laypersons of type B are those who function as "voluntary clergy" and find their primary interest not in the world which provides their live-lihood but in a ministry within the local church. Their primary interest is in the church as gathered, *ecclesia*.[5] I was clearly a type B layperson. It is comforting to know that you fit in a category!

In his careful study of the layperson in the first three centuries of the church, George Williams shows that it was not only in the gathered phase *(ecclesia)* but especially in the disperson life *(diaspora)* that Christians spread the word. The pagan Celcius admitted in the second century that it was the "wool-workers, cobblers, laundry-workers and the most illiterate and bucolic yokels" who carried the gospel forth, even more than the bishops, the apologists and the theologians.[6]

The only true picture of the church is a moving picture: a daily or weekly gathering and then dispersion, gathering and then dispersion. The church is present in the world in the person of the church member, especially layperson type A. It was the laity who reached the Roman world with the gospel, and the two billion unreached people in the modern world can be reached only if every Christian is mobilized. The lost cannot be evangelized or discipled by professional supported workers alone. Fulfilling the Great Commission *requires* an equipped laity. And theology of mission for the equipped layperson must take seriously the unique position where God in his sovereignty has placed that man or woman in the world. He or she will need to be nourished for that position in the world (a matter addressed in chapter six).

If type A laypersons (*diaspora* Christians) are undernourished, type B laypersons (*ecclesia* Christians) are undervalued. Both need to be equipped. The church has largely concentrated its lay training programs on the needs of type B laypeople by giving them skills for teaching Sunday school, doing visitation evangelism or small group leadership training. But equipping is much more than giving people skills for ministry. That is one of the myths about equipping that must be de-bunked. Equipping is more concerned with character formation than skills or information. W. E. Vine helpfully points out that the Greek word for "equipping," *katartizō*, "points out the path of progress."[7] Equip-ping implies a journey toward a distant destination. Character is not formed quickly and rarely by taking courses.

If we took the training and equipping of these two types of laity as seriously as we have taken the training of the professional ministry, there would be a revolution for Christ in the world. Gibbs and Morton suggest that the thawing out of "the frozen assets of the Church would be for us like the discovery of a new continent or a new element."[8]

Dashing home with lunch bucket and toolbox in hand to take in an elders meeting, I discovered something else. It was much easier to begin a lay ministry than it was to stop being a clergyman. "Clergy" is not so much a matter of position or being paid or having a title or receiving a certain status in the community. It is a whole mentality, a mentality of feeling responsible to provide the vision for the church, of leading the church, even running it. It is this feeling of indispensability that drives us to assume a responsibility for the church which rightfully belongs only to the Head, to Christ. I have witnessed this mentality not only in myself but in tentmaking elders serving in plural leadership who thought they were functioning in a nonclerical structure. In contrast, I have seen pastors in traditional one-man-minister structures who saw themselves as servant leaders appointed not to enlist the laity as their assistants but to liberate each layperson for his or her own ministry.

The months and years of working in the world in the church were for me hammer and heat on the anvil of life. I was being forged at one and the same time both as a layperson and also as a renewed pastoral leader. Far from turning me against leadership, the experience showed me the true place and spirit of leadership in the church.

I was, I admit, not an ordinary layperson. I realized this every time I sat down to lunch with the electricians and the drywall tapers. I knew too much about some things and too little about others. My seminary training and my experience as a pastor had, in some measure, separated me from these men. I recalled having read many years before a penetrating passage in Abbé Michonneau's *Revolution in a City Parish* on the problem of "clerical culture." He said, "Our seminary training in the classics, philosophy and theology has put us in a class apart. . . . Usually it means that we feel compelled to surround ourselves with those who will understand our thought and our speech, and who have tastes like our own. . . . We are living in another world, a tidy clerical and philo-

sophical world. It is time to come down to earth!"[9] He was writing out
of a Catholic worker-priest context but I knew it applied to me. It was
time for me to come down to earth!

If only it could have been done without pain! But equipping always
involves sacrifice. There is always a thorn. There is no easy way to do
ministry, whether as supported or tentmaking, whether in the church for
God as a professional Christian or in the world for God as a Christian
professional.

A New Spirituality

It is perfectly obvious to every nonprofessional minister that the average
working layperson spends most of his or her time providing for the
family. The average homemaking mother or father is almost entirely
absorbed by that task. As a pastor I had never fully appreciated this. My
repeated calls for involvement in this or that church activity betrayed
that I did not understand the rhythm of the lay life.

Since the laity spends an enormous amount of time working inside
or outside the home, their "church time" must be only a fraction of their
life for God. Unless we equip the laity to live all of life for God, Christianity will degenerate into mere religion. I had to learn that true spirituality is hammering nails for God and praying before a precise saw cut.
Glorifying God is going home and listening to and enjoying the news
of my three children as they recite their day's activities. The secret of
having a single eye to God—a matter to which we will return—is to
leave no part of one's bodily life in the dark (Lk 11:33-35).

This came home to me one day when I was particularly discouraged
as a tentmaker. It was the old thorn problem again. I felt that I had three
full-time jobs: carpentry, church leadership and my family. Neither the
job nor the ministry was going very well at the time. Probably I had been
expecting too much fulfillment in my daily work because I seemed to
be going nowhere. At the time I was framing in a basement room for
a Christian brother. "Bob," I said, "what do you think I should do with
my life?" Undoubtedly Joseph must have asked this in prison in Egypt,
perhaps even when he was viceregent for Pharaoh, until he saw the end
from the beginning and the hand of God in his life (Gen 45:5, 7-8).

Bob knew exactly what I was thinking because he too had been learning to see vocation and calling as larger than work and ministry. He reminded me about Moses. "Never forget," he said, "that Moses had two useless careers—one for forty years as an administrator in Pharaoh's court and another for forty years as a shepherd in Midian. But God gloriously redeemed both useless careers to make him a shepherd and administrator of God's people." I'm not sure Moses' first two careers were useless. But I am sure that it is only with the eye of faith that we can see the usefulness of our life at any given moment.

Bob equipped me that day. He called me once again to live for God where I *was* and to learn contentment.

Equipping is in the end a pastoral task. The Greek word for equipping, *katartismos,* is used as a noun only once—in Ephesians 4:12. But the word has an interesting medical history in classical Greek. To equip is to put a bone or a part of the human body into right relationship with the other parts of the body so that every part fits thoroughly. It means to realign a dislocated limb. What Bob did for me that day was to put me back in joint.

I thought I was well on the way to being an equipper when I took up my hammer and saw. But when I set them down again, to re-enter the professional ministry as a teaching elder at Marineview Chapel, I had even more to learn. Equipping starts with the equipper getting equipped. And complete equipping requires the environment of the local church, as our study of the context of Ephesians 4:12 will now show.

2. The Abolition of the Laity: Biblical Foundations

George Bernard Shaw once said that every profession is a conspiracy against the laity. Although professional clergy do sometimes distance themselves from the laity—sometimes intentionally—this is contrary to their true calling.

Through an exegetical study of Ephesians 4:1-16, we will discover what is required to reduce the gap, or to eliminate it altogether. We must measure the adequacy of lay training programs against God's grand plan for equipping all the saints. It is not primarily a *program* that is needed, but an *environment.* An environment is the sum total of the social, relational and spiritual attitudes and factors in a society or group that influences what the individual thinks of him or herself and what he or she does. The word "atmosphere" is close to what we mean. What most needs to be equipped is not the laity, but their environment, the local church. When that is done, the leadership will not be dragged down, as is sometimes thought, to the level of the laity. All the people of God—both so-called clergy and so-called laity—will be elevated to their true dignity as ministers of Jesus Christ. The laity, as conceived by the church today, will be abolished altogether.

But all too often being a member of a church is like joining the badminton club in the community center near my home. Gail and I knew that we needed some exercise. While I am hopelessly unathletic (I tend to meditate in the middle of a competitive game), Gail is fiercely competitive. But badminton would be new for both of us. We would get equipped and involved together.

Not knowing the official badminton color, I bought some blue gym shorts and reactivated an unused blue tee shirt. At a sale I picked up a pair of runners. They had fluorescent green, blue and yellow stripes. (My children will not be seen with me when I wear them.) Salvaging two discarded badminton racquets from the garbage can of a local private school, Gail and I set out to join the club. We were fully equipped, or so we thought.

Arriving a little late we poked our heads in the gym. Everyone was dressed in white from head to toe. And everyone knew exactly what to do. Everyone, that is, except us! We watched them popping birds between their legs and over their shoulders. It was poetry in motion.

Looking for the person in charge, our eyes eventually settled on an imposing lady who seemed to be running things. "Excuse me," I said, "we are new here and we don't know very much about badminton."

"You don't?" she said condescendingly. "Then what are you doing here?"

If we could have left gracefully, we would have. Instead, rather than imposing ourselves on the "professionals," we decided to put our names up on the playing schedule. We agreed that on the day we were no longer chosen as playing partners we would leave.

Now we swim on Tuesday evenings.

Trying to join this club gave me a new empathy for people trying to find their place in the body of Christ. The experience strengthened my resolve to abolish the laity. Joining that badminton club is all too close to the experience many people have when trying to join the church and to find their place in ministry. This pitiful badminton club did not suffer from overleadership, but from underleadership. If the laity are to be equipped—and thereby abolished—we will need better leadership and more of it. Each person in the club was doing his or her own thing, which is light-years away from the condition Paul speaks of where the body grows and builds itself up in love "as each part does its work" (Eph 4:16).

What an Equipping Church Looks Like

What my experience in the badminton club and my study of Ephesians 4 have confirmed is simply this: The club needs to be equipped in its fundamental life, its environment, its structure, its leadership and goals, if its members are ever to be equipped. Our first task is to see that the church is equipped.

The passage under study is not actually a passage about equipping. "To equip the saints for the work of the ministry" (Eph 4:12 RSV) appears in a theological context dealing with the unity of the church. We must hear the central message of the passage. Equipping is not a thing to be valued in itself, but is an instrument of God's grand plans for his people, especially that they may be one.

In studying this passage we will ask the text two questions. What does an equipping environment look like? and Who are the equippers?

If we start where the Bible does, rather than where we wish the Bible did, we must ask what a fully equipped church looks like. Even a quick survey of Ephesians 4:1-16 reveals that such a church is characterized by a profound unity, a unity different from anything we can find in the world.

Ephesians 4:1 is the watershed of the whole book. From this summit, Paul looks back through chapters 1—3, which tell us *who we are,* and anticipates chapters 4—6, where we learn *what we are to do* about who we are. The first half of the letter is doctrine; the second half duty. Chapters 1—3 are *kērygma,* a proclamation; chapters 4—6 are *didachē,* teaching. Paul moves from the indicative—what we are—to the imperative—what we must do. The letter moves from being to doing, from grace to activity. That is the Lord's way. And it is essential to see that ministry flows from our identity in Christ; it does not come from our identity in the world.

Unity of Calling

Simply put, vocation or calling (they are the same concept) is what you do with who you are in Christ. Every believer has been called to be Jesus' disciple and to serve in the kingdom of God. This is the "one hope" to which we are "called" (4:4). Fundamentally, then, there is no clergy-laity distinction. All are called of God. The "secret call" of the preacher or pastor does not make him or her more called than the carpenter; and the nuclear physicist that lives out his life for God in society is not less called than the priest. To make this point embarrassingly clear, Markus Barth says that the whole church, the community of all the saints together, "is the *clergy* appointed by God for a ministry to and for the world."[1]

According to God's grand plan, we are called to a ministry that flows out from our life in God and into the world. Paul says, "As a prisoner for the Lord, then, I urge you to live a life worthy of the calling [vocation] you have received" (4:1).

"There is one body and one Spirit—just as you were called to one hope when you were called—one Lord, one faith, one baptism; one God and Father of all" (4:4-6). Paul here links the unique sevenfold unity of believers to the unity within the Godhead. Just as the Father, Son and Spirit are three yet one, so believers are first of all to think of themselves as members of one body, then as members within it.

This theme of unity undergirds the whole passage. Unity is *given* as a part of our calling, and it is to be maintained as we "make every effort to *keep* the unity of the Spirit" (4:3). But it is also to be *attained* as God's people are equipped through the building up of the body "until we all reach unity in the faith and in the knowledge of the Son of God" (4:13). Between the given unity of our inheritance in Christ and the attained unity of maturity in Christ is the equipping task.

Unity of Ministry

What is remarkable when we further explore this unity in the church is the fact that it exists not in spite of diversity, but because of it. Ephesians 4:1-16 moves thematically from *one* calling (4:1) to the *many* expressions of grace (4:7) and *many* gifts for ministry (4:11), and then ties these all together to the *one* common goal of maturity in Christ (4:13).

It is the differences themselves which, when properly equipped, contribute to the deeper attained unity of maturity. In the body of Christ, unity is the opposite of uniformity. Not only is the clergy-laity distinction absent from a church made up of one people, but every one of the various ministries is essential to the unity of the whole.

Every member of the body is indispensable. Only as *each part does its work* (4:16) can the body grow and attain its goal of maturity and unity in Christ. To this end, grace has been given to each one of us (4:7). Each of us *becomes* a minister of that particular grace which we have been given for the sake of the church. Thus the gifts of the Spirit for ministry are not mere functions or activities carried out by the members. The gifts are *people,* the men and women whom you are connected in Christ.

Not surprisingly, then, when Paul speaks of gifts for ministry in verse 11, giving apostles, prophets, evangelists and pastor-teachers as examples, the emphasis is not on these gifts but on these people. In receiving the grace of Christ we *become* ministers. We don't *have* a ministry; we *are* one. Grace has been given—that is the indicative. You will minister—that is the imperative. God's gifts are people endowed with a special grace from Christ for ministry. Because you *have* the gift of grace from Christ, you *are* a gift to the body. Seen this way, ministry is a natural and delightful duty.

In a church that recognizes that every member is given grace from Christ, every member will be prized, every ministry will be appreciated, every differing experience of the grace of Christ will be treasured. Such an environment will communicate "we need you!"—even if you wear fluorescent-striped runners!

In a business or other organization, the manager uses people with skills and abilities to accomplish a goal. The manager's dilemma arises when nurturing his workers comes into conflict with accomplishing the goals of the enterprise.[2] In the church, however, the goal *is* the body and its upbuilding. Therefore the nurture of each member is more important than the function and task of the member.

When Richard Halverson, as pastor, surveyed the membership of the First Presbyterian Church of Hollywood, he learned a "significant" lesson. It required only 365 persons to maintain the *program* of the 7,000-member church.[3] But in light of Paul's teaching in Ephesians 4, it requires 7,000 persons to maintain and upbuild that *body.* Its environment should have communicated that fundamental fact.

Unity in Common Life

The word *together* appears so frequently and in such innovative ways in this letter that it deserves special study. Paul uses the Greek prefix *sun* ("with" or "together") and joins this prefix to a number of key words to describe the practical impossibility of being in Christ alone. What is translated into English as a phrase is one compound word in the original: we are "made . . . alive with Christ" (2:5); "seated . . . with him in the heavenly realms" (2:6); "fellow citizens with God's people" (2:19); "joined together" (2:21); "being built together" (2:22); "heirs together," "members together," "sharers together" (3:6); and, reaching a climax, "joined and held together by every supporting ligament" (4:16). Paul is using the strongest possible language—indeed he is creating new language—to describe the interdependence of every member in the body. We can no more disconnect ourselves from other members and remain healthy than we can disconnect the ligaments from the bones or try to live without veins and arteries.

The word sometimes translated "joints" (Phillips) or "ligaments" (NIV) in 4:16 does not mean that certain members of the body have the special charisma of making all the connections for others. I once thought this was the pastor's job. The root meaning of the word suggests "touch" or "contact." Paul is saying that every member *in his or her contact with other members* supplies something the body needs. Markus Barth translates this verse: "He [Christ] provides sustenance to it through every contact."[4]

In order to be an equipping environment, therefore, the local church must be structured for relationships. Instead of coming to hear a performance or sitting on a committee, new members should find themselves drawn into a network of relationships. And their involvement (as should be made clear) needs to be seen as making a positive contribution to the health of the total community. New members should not need to wait for several years to see if they will fit in and whether other people will choose to "play" the game with them. The milieu must communicate that they are needed and connected.

Unity in Purpose

The climax of Ephesians 4:1-16 is also the goal of the equipping ministry. This goal is much more than gaining a skill or accumulating knowledge; it is nothing less than maturity in Christ. "We will in all things grow up into him who is the Head, that is, Christ" (4:15). "Until we all reach unity in the faith and in the knowledge of the Son of God and become mature, attaining to the full measure of the fullness of Christ" (4:13). Equipping has no less a goal than this: the maturity of both individuals and the whole church. Maturity is the master concept of the Christian life and the ultimate goal of equipping.

As defined in this passage, maturity is relational humility (4:2), rather than self-realization; doctrinal certainty (4:14), rather than shifting innovativeness; and interdependence (4:16), rather than independence. All this is "from him," but it requires that each part do its work (4:16).

Thus, far from being a diversion, the discovery of the theme of unity— unity in calling, unity in ministry, unity in common life and unity in purpose—provides the theological setting for the heart of equipping. It gives us a game plan. The theme of unity in Ephesians 4 suggests that we are to be concerned not merely with individual members but with the whole environment of the local church. The environment itself must communicate that the whole body together has clerical status. Which is the same as saying that it has the honor of the true laity of God. The whole environment of the church must communicate the unity of an organism rather than the unity of an organization.

How fundamental the environment is for equipping was shown by Stephen Clark in an original work on the nature of Christian community.[5] He shows that environmental factors are more basic than institutional factors in Christian growth. The task of church leaders is to shape the environment. They are environmental engineers. My badminton club through its entire social environment gave me a negative equipping message. The church as the body of Christ should communicate that every member is interrelated to other members and indispensable. The message the church conveys by its environment communicates more clearly than any formal public pronouncement. Citing the example of the radical change in sexual morality in North America, Clark shows that people were not changed by public teaching, which was often against the so-called new morality, but by the total environment.[6]

Advertising works by creating an environment. It is one of the most conspicuous but least regarded of our contemporary social forces. Experts estimate that at least fourteen hundred times a day our eyes and ears are assailed by advertising.[7] Modifying a line from Marshall McLuhan, we could say that not merely is the medium the message, the milieu is the medium. Or at least that was the case with my badminton club.

The most important thing we can do, then, toward equipping all the saints for ministry is to shape the environment in unity and complementarity so that every member "hears" from the environment the message: not *you* but *we;* not your personal self-development, but building up the body as "each part does its work" (4:16).

Who Is the Equipper?

Frank Tillapaugh is one of the few contemporary authors who tries to think through the matter of releasing or liberating the laity. Given that there are so many more laypeople than pastor-teachers, Tillapaugh argues in *The Church Unleashed* that the scriptural pattern is that "pastor-teachers are to train lay men and women to minister to the world. They in turn are to train others and the work continues."[8]

This is surely one of the most believed but least practiced principles of the contemporary church. It implies that the function of professional ministers is to make themselves dispensable by equipping others for ministry. They are called to equip the saints for the work of the ministry,

ministry of and by the saints.

The two principles that undergird this entire book are these: First, church leadership is called *primarily* to an equipping ministry. This is not a sideline to preaching or counseling, but the raison d'être of the pastor-teacher. Second, equipping the saints does not mean harnessing the laity for the felt needs or institutional tasks of the church nor harnessing the laity to assist the pastor with certain delegated ministries. The saints are to be equipped *for their own ministry.* The pastor should not be trying to replicate his or her own ministry but to release theirs. In the process, the laity, as a separate category of ministry in the body of Christ, is abolished.

That this kind of ministry would revolutionize the contemporary church there can be little doubt. But before proceeding we must be quite certain that it is true to Scripture. We must now press the text (again Eph 4:1-16) with a second question: Who are the equippers in the New Testament church?

Surveying the passage, we discover that there is not one category of equipping minister in the New Testament church but several. I call these the underequippers. These include the elders, deacons, pastor-teachers, apostles, prophets and evangelists—all those we commonly call "ministers" and "pastors." More important than anything done by these underequippers, however, is what is done by the Head of the body, the Ultimate Equipper.

The Ultimate Equipper

Behind all the wonders Paul describes in Ephesians is God. It is God who calls (4:1); God in Christ who apportions grace to each (4:7); God who gives special word-ministers (apostles, prophets, evangelists, pastor-teachers); God who gives growth in the body. But he accomplishes all this through his Anointed One —the Christ—and this has a number of consequences.

Jesus is the giver of gifts and graces of ministry. The context of the teaching on gifts in Ephesians 4 is the completed work of Christ. Endowing the laity of God with ministry gifts is not a divine afterthought. Ephesians 4:8-11 presents a picture of a triumphant king who has liberated captives and shares the spoils of victory with his people. Taking the spoils of that victory with him, he "ascended" to heaven to fill the whole universe (4:10). Paul quotes here the Greek version of Psalm 68:18 which reads, "he *gave* gifts to men"; the Hebrew version reads, "he *received* gifts from men." But whether the picture is that of a triumphant king in procession receiving gifts from his new subjects or the ascended Christ receiving gifts from his Father and bestowing them on men, the image is one of gifts coming from a completed battle and a sovereign Lord.

Jesus' long-range plan is to fill the universe with his glory. His short-range plan is to do this by filling the church. He pours out on the church the spoils of his cosmic battle on the cross by giving himself to his people. Each of us is a fraction of his image. He has apportioned grace to each of us (4:7). Therefore, spiritual gifts are gifts *from* Christ and *of* Christ. Rather than calling them "spiritual gifts," we might better call them "grace-gifts" or "Christ-gifts."

Christ provides for the equipment of the body by giving special ministers. While in 1 Corinthians 12:4-31 the gifts of the Spirit are "charisms" or grace-gifts *(charismata)* for service, in Ephesians Paul speaks of the gifts in terms of *persons* who have received various gifts of ministry. (Since Paul obviously considers these named "gifted" ministers of first importance to the church, we will return shortly to the question of whether the listing of apostles, prophets, evangelists and pastor-teachers is exclusively a statement about the founding ministers of the church, or whether they reflect ministers in the church today.)

We must not think that these gifted ministers are the only ones bestowed on the church. This is abundantly clear from the purpose for which these ministers were given: they are "to equip the saints for works of service, for building up the body of Christ."[9] According to F. F. Bruce, rendering the verse in this way is supported by a change of preposition in the Greek, thus: "Unto *[pros]* the equipment of the saints for *[eis]* the work of service."[10] Bruce concludes that "the gifts enumerated in verse 11 do not monopolize the Church's ministry; their function rather is so to help and direct the Church that all the members may perform their several ministries for the good of the whole." Then, quoting E. K.

Simpson, he adds, "In the theocracy of grace there is in fact no laity."[11]

In short, the equipping ministry of the Lord effectively abolishes what we call the laity by providing for every member to become engaged in ministry. The notion that one person could so embody the charismatic gifts of ministry for the church that he or she might be called *the* minister is not only a practical heresy. It is an affront to the intention of the Head Equipper.

Christ is the head of the body and is personally responsible for equipping the body. In Ephesians 4:15 and elsewhere Paul emphasizes that the church is not a body of Christians but the body of Christ, with Jesus as the Head (Eph 1:23; 5:23; Col 1:18). It is not primarily an organization but an organism. And the Head of this organism is not in the clouds, but in intimate and living connection with the body. Jesus lives among us and in us; we are his temple and his body.

There is a direct and living connection between the Head and every member of the body. Nothing in this passage or any other suggests that Christ has delegated his headship to certain church leaders who are responsible for the ministry and the life of others. No church leader in the New Testament is even ever called the head of a local body. That title is reserved for Jesus. The head does not tell the hand to tell the foot what to do. The head is connected directly with the foot. Therefore people find their ministries not by being directed by the leaders but by being motivated and equipped and directed by the Head himself.

The church, then, is not a democracy but a theocracy. Jesus, as Head, is King. Gideon in the tribal confederation of the Old Covenant, wisely rejected being king with the words, "The LORD will rule over you" (Judg 8:23). The book of Judges ends with the statement that "in those days Israel had no king; everyone did as he saw fit" (Judg 21:25). The problem was with the second half of the statement, not the first half.

In other words, the church is not a hierarchy but a monarchy. The will of the Head is not mediated through various levels of government (pastors, elders or deacons, small group leaders and so on), but comes directly to all his subjects.

Christ himself is the goal of the equipping ministry. All the saints are to be equipped with the express goal of "attaining to the whole measure of the fullness of Christ" (Eph 4:13). We are to "grow up into him who is the Head" (4:15).

What a relief it is for the human underequippers to know this. Their major function is not to run the church but to get every member of the body *to relate to the Head for himself or herself.* The goal of equipping is not to make people dependent on the leaders but dependent on the Head. This is the highest possible calling. It requires the strongest possible leadership in the church to lead people in such a way that they do not become dependent on the human leaders. Sometimes the church which is being led and equipped in this way is portrayed as a leaderless group, each person doing his own thing, much like my badminton club. But in truth, equipping, directing people to find their life and future in Christ himself, makes the highest claim on leadership.

Ancient doctors spoke of the brain as the acropolis, the supreme power of the body; they even compared the nervous system to a tree growing out of the brain.[12] But Paul said that the body grows *into* the Head, and the body's nourishment and growth are supplied by the Head through every connection or "joint" between the believers (4:16).

Picture a situation that actually happened in a Brethren assembly some years ago. In the course of the Sunday morning announcements, one of the elders said this: "Those with a burden for the work will be meeting on Monday night at eight in the lounge." Over the years, by common consent, this phrase—"those with a burden for the work"— had become a not-so-secret announcement to tell the elders where they were to meet. After all, the elders were the only appointed leaders with a burden for the work—or so they thought.

But two young men, one who was already preaching on street corners, also had a burden for the work and went to the lounge at eight. Not only were they given a cold reception, but the meeting was immediately changed to another room. The elders hoped to lose the two young hopefuls on the way. But the young men were tenacious. In desperation the chairman canceled the meeting altogether and the two young men went home frustrated and hurt.

How different it would have been if the elders had believed that Jesus was the Head, not they. Had they welcomed the God-given concern of these younger brothers, awkward as it was, they could have sent them home nourished with their counsel and prayers. Lacking any official clergyman or paid professional, they yet behaved in a manner comparable to the worst of the ecclesiastical reigning monarchs.

Often the problem is that while we *say* Christ is the King of the church, we treat him, like the Queen of England, as a figurehead, a constitutional monarch who reigns but does not rule. Church leaders may assume the throne, while claiming that they honor the reign of the King himself. In contrast, Paul calls us to nurture an environment in the local church that says to every member, "We want to discover why God has joined you to this particular local body."

The Underequippers
Leading ministers, whether apostles or pastor-teachers or plural elders, have the primary function of bringing people under the authority of

"From now on we're going to operate as a theocracy . . . and I'm Theo."

Christ and the Scriptures. They will not account for every member of the flock. (Jesus is the bishop of their souls.) They will give account for what they have done with the flock. They are not intermediaries in the chain of command, representing the will of an absent or silent Lord. Rather their task as "underequippers" is to nurture people in Jesus' leadership and headship.

Perhaps that is why, significantly, all the special ministers listed are ministers of the Word. Apostles preach the Word and new churches are founded. Prophets speak God's Word to concrete situations. Evangelists preach the gospel. The pastor-teacher nurtures a local congregation in the Word.

We must pause for a moment to consider a question which often arises concerning apostles. In Ephesians 2:20 Paul calls apostles the Lord's foundational gifts to the church. Does he mean that after the first century, that is, after the church had been founded, there would no longer be apostles in the church because they would then be unnecessary? It is certainly true that the founding apostles were unique in being directly commissioned by Christ. But the term gains a more inclusive sense even during the period of the formation of the New Testament itself. Others, not directly commissioned by Christ but associated with the original apostles and doing the same work, are included among the "apostles." Among these are Timothy and Silvanus (1 Thess 1:1; 2:7) and Andronicus and Junias (Rom 16:7). There is certainly some sense in which the missionary gift today is a continuation of the apostolic gift, even though the primary apostolic function of true witness to Jesus is now performed by the Scriptures of the New Testament.

In his excellent treatment of this subject Arnold Bittlinger points out that apostles were called of God, singled out by the church, recognized by the church at large and confirmed by apostolic signs. They are "empowered to maintain or bring to birth the relationships between Christ and his churches."[13] It is a normal ministry that is always needed, as Calvin himself maintained in his *Institutes* (4. 3. 4).

Concerning the prophets, they too had a unique role in the church prior to the formation of the New Testament (Eph 3:5). Their authoritative interpretation of the Old Testament as fulfilled in Christ was foundational to the New Testament church. However, speech under direct inspiration of the Spirit did not come to an end when the Scriptures were canonized. In this age of the Spirit (Acts 2:17), the servants of the Lord, both men and women, will continue to bring words from the Lord, applying the truth of the Scripture to life. There is not a single verse in the New Testament which, taken in context, suggests that the gift of prophecy is gone for good, or irrelevant to the church with its Bible in hand.[14]

Amazingly, prophecy, in this general sense of bringing an inspired word to another, is potentially everyone's gift since Pentecost. With the Spirit in our hearts and the Bible in hand, any believer may equip his brother or sister by bringing a word for "strengthening, encouragement or comfort" (1 Cor 14:3).

Evangelists are mentioned in the New Testament only in Ephesians 4. But the idea of proclaiming the good news is a favorite one of Luke and is close to the idea of "witness" in John's writings. It would be shortchanging the New Testament to limit evangelists to mass evangelists or merely to personal witnesses. Regardless of the form this ministry takes today, it is essential for introducing people to the whole message of Christ.

Pastor-teachers (or pastors and teachers) are those who "tend the flock of God" by both personal care and biblical instruction. Of all the designated underequippers, the pastor-teacher comes closest to what, in the pastoral epistles, are called "elders" and "bishops." These were settled ministers in local congregations. They worked with other pastor-teachers, as there was always more than one in each location, and one of their qualifications was to be "able to teach" (1 Tim 3:2).

From the passage being studied it is obvious that whatever leadership the church has has no greater mandate than the one given to the first leaders, namely, to equip the saints—all of them—for ministry both in the church and in the world. The leaders will do this primarily in the context of exercising their own gifts. But the leading servants (ministers—it is the same word in Greek) are to be servant leaders.

The matter of equipping the pastor will be taken up in chapter seven. For the moment, we must note that there is no biblical or theological justification for regarding church leaders as peculiarly called of God to minister holy things or to be "full-time" for God, while considering the layperson, who serves God in both church and world, as having a lesser call or no call at all. The part-time lay minister is a misnomer.

The church needs specially gifted leaders, highly qualified and trained servant-ministers, recognized elders and equipping ministers. But there is no room at all in the New Testament church for a hierarchy of callings. The call of God comes to every believer who has ears to hear. This call finds believers in a variety of situations. Indeed, our life situation is so important that Paul counseled the Corinthians not to leave the situation they were in when Christ first called them (1 Cor 7:17, 20). We are to walk worthy of this call where we are. Oswald Chambers puts this enigmatically when he says, "Never allow the thought—'I am of no use where I am'; because you certainly can be of no use where you are not."[15]

Since we are all "joints," connected to others whom we may choose either to edify or ignore, equipping is every believer's task. At the point of our interaction with other believers, we have this choice to make: Will I seek my own fulfillment or will I build up the body by building up this sister or brother? The primary underequippers are to model equipping for us, but we can never delegate this completely to them. To be God's own possession is our dignity (Eph 1:14). Our ministry flows out of this identity. By the grace of God we have been chosen, appointed and anointed, a special people, a holy nation, priests to our God. We are all clergy—priestly ministers.

This comes home to me afresh every time I look at my antique clay oil lamp over my desk. Some people think I collect junk; they have no idea of how valuable this oil lamp is to me. It originally came from Hebron, Israel. It is as old as the reign of David. I admit that it looks like an ash tray. The lamps of that period were open-topped, like a small bowl with a slight flange in the lip at one place for the wick. Instead of a wick, a cigarette could rest there just as easily.

How could I assume that a priest, officiating at a wedding in our church, would know the value of this lamp to me? I can picture him waiting with the groom in my study, this visiting colleague, nervously taking his last drag and then unceremoniously ramming the butt of his cigarette into thirty centuries of antiquity.

Early Sunday morning it was there to greet me, that butt, broken like an old stove pipe, bent over the lip of the lamp. I was righteously indignant. My lamp, like the laity, had not been given the dignity and esteem which it was due. He had profaned my treasure. I thought of leaving a sign with the text "What God has cleansed, you must not call common" or perhaps, "This is a vessel fit for honor."

The laity, as a social and religious category lacking honor and respect, was abolished when Jesus ascended and gave gifts of ministry to his people. Henceforth, the laity is a dignified vocation. And the environment of the church must be designed to equip all members for this high calling.

But to warn future offenders, I settled for "Please don't butt your cigarettes in my oil lamp."

Part II
Structures for Equipping the Laity

3. A Most Unruly and Chaotic Little Bible School

Jake and Marion had just returned from the most recent training seminar to hit our town. Little did they know that they had just returned *to* the best training center they could find: the local church.

Their slightly glazed eyes told the story. They were cloistered for the conference in a hotel that exuded hedonism. Moving from sumptuous meal to plenary session to small group, they went through a program they said was "professional." Some of the biggest names in North America were there. As they spoke of intimate sharing of life secrets in a hot tub with people they had never seen before—and would never see again—I recalled Bonhoeffer's warning that there is nothing so dangerous as the feeling of fellowship gained on a retreat of short duration.

They had been "trained." But the next night in our evangelistic Bible study group they found themselves in a hot debate with a bitter but seeking non-Christian. Marion later described the evening as oppressive and "totally unnerving," a time of spiritual warfare. Flashing back to the spiritual high at the hotel, she openly wondered how advanced our group was. The attack had come from a woman going through a ghastly divorce. Marion would have to face her again—every week. This is the church. And this is also the best place to be trained in ministry.

Going to School at the Local Church

The best structure for equipping every Christian is already in place. It predates the seminary and the weekend seminar and will outlast both. In the New Testament no other nurturing and equipping agency is offered other than the local church. In the New Testament church, as in the ministry of Jesus, people learned in the furnace of life, in a relational, living, working and ministering context.

In their masterful study *God's Frozen People,* Gibbs and Morton describe the intensive learning environment of the first- and second-century church:

> There was plenty of theological study and discussion. Indeed it could be argued that in no subsequent age was there so much theological education. But *it was carried out in the whole body of the church.* It was not a specialist study for the training of the professional servants of the church. Paul's letters were not written to be studied by ordinands in theological colleges; they were written to be read in church and to be studied by all the members of the church. . . . It was an unruly and chaotic training in theology but it was open to all and all could contribute. . . . It was carried on in the midst of the noisy life of the church and was shared by others, merchants, slaves and women, all of whom made their contribution. It was a theological education for the people of the church—it was lay, not clerical.[1]

Scripture does not preclude other structures for training people, such as parachurch training programs and seminaries. I owe too much to the seminary to snub it. Training programs, Bible schools and prepackaged equipping seminars all contribute to the fullness of equipping that is available today. But they must never be primary.

Having completed two years of theological education in an excellent

Canadian seminary, I was, as the philosopher Alfred North Whitehead once said, "overladen with inert ideas."[2] But God called me simultaneously to two great equipping arenas: marriage and the church. Luther once said these were God's two great gifts for our sanctification.

Taking up leadership in a small, struggling inner-city church while completing my theological studies over a longer period of time, I found that theology came alive. The Bible spoke to my daily experience. Dealing with families living in dismal flats heated by toasters and ovens, moving furniture and moving people, I found myself in a true parish. For *paroichos* means "a people on the move," and I had some families that were moving every month. To heal the heart of that wounded city, Montreal, God's people—his laity—would have to be equipped. No professional mission or missionary could do it.

Equipping was an idea I was anxious to put to use—the one idea that was not inert. I set out to become not the minister but the facilitator and trainer of ministers. In the process I got equipped too. I commuted every day to a downtown seminary; but it seemed to be in a world apart. The real learning was what I was discovering in actual local church life and ministry. It was the best little Bible school going. It was also a little bit unruly and chaotic.

Scripture and my experience conspired to teach me the reasons for concentrating on the local church as the primary equipping structure. First, *Scripture assumes the local church* is the context for growing to maturity in Christ. No other training agency was foreseen. Equipping all the saints for the work of the ministry, as we have already seen in Ephesians 4, takes place within the body of Christ.

Second, the genius of learning in the local church is that it is *relational,* for the church is a community designed by God for learning. Most people would not be together but for Christ. Relationships in the body of Christ are often not ones we would have chosen. That very mix of unlikely people becomes under God a special incentive to learn ministry.

Third, because the church is a rhythm of gathering and dispersing, training is inevitably *related to life.* What is going on in one's family, one's work and one's neighborhood intersects with life together in the body. And so it should if learning is to be maximized.

Fourth, every local church has *all the spiritual gifts* needed to be complete in Christ. The Head sees to that. In the church, therefore, in contrast to specialized ministries which center around singularly gifted people, believers are exposed to the full charismatic expression of Christ's ministry. Often the member with the gift of helps or mercy may have the greatest influence on a growing Christian.

Fifth, the church is a *multigenerational family*. One of the things that makes the church the church is the presence of children, parents, grandparents and other adults. Repeated references to the church as a household, family or fellowship underscore the connection between the church as the New Covenant community and the family as a covenant community. How can we learn to be New Covenant ministers outside of a family context?

Sixth, what really counts in local church life is not knowledge but *maturity of character*. That is not only the goal of ministry (Col 1:28), but a practical requirement of church leaders (1 Tim 3; Tit 1). J. Andrew Kirk complains of the dichotomy between the standards for ordained and nonordained leadership. The ordained person, he argues, is taken from the bottom of the pile and reintroduced, after suitable theological processing, at the top; while the nonordained person emerges only after being proved in life and in actual ministry in the local church.[3]

Seventh, it takes *time*, lots of time, to form character and train for ministry. Commenting on the need for longer on-the-job training, Peter Davids says "the failure to allow time for such spiritual/character qualifications to develop may be one of the reasons for the stagnation of the Western church."[4] Remaining with a particular local church for ten or twenty years will bear a different kind of fruit than a three-year intensive program.

Professional Training Models

The secret of good medicine is accurate diagnosis. In chapter one we saw that three pressures bearing on the church from without and within created the clergy-laity distinction: secularism, sacerdotalism and sacramentalism. Here we will explore a fourth—professionalism.

The professional training of the supported minister usually serves as the model for lay training programs in the local church. Replicating this model, many local churches now have Bible schools in their buildings or short seminary-type courses which offer a diluted version of the professional training experience. A number of large churches in the United States offer very substantial training courses in pastoring, evangelism or church growth. But, as a *Christianity Today* article suggested, the lecturers, faculty and staff "deal with details of how that particular super church performs its diverse ministries."[5] Fortunately, there are some constructive examples of how the school approach can be fully integrated into the equipping of the laity both for life in the church and ministry outside it. (An example is the school offered by the Church of the Savior, Washington, D.C.)

The most articulate defense of adult education in the local church has been given by Elton Trueblood, the eminent Quaker. "Education is too good to limit to the young," he says. "Adult education is the big thing in the church. It is not a decoration, it is the centerpiece."[6] With that I wholeheartedly agree. But Trueblood also wrote, in the *Incendiary Fellowship,* that "the congregation must, accordingly, be reconstructed into the pattern of a small theological seminary with the pastor as the professor."[7] This is an exciting but dangerous idea.

Since most lay training programs are patterned after the seminary model, it is crucial for us to be aware of the seminary's inherent weakness in practical theology. (In due course I will suggest some alternative models.) Typically, the seminary is residential, university-modeled, uses a four-part classical curriculum, and is classroom-based and content-oriented. Fortunately, significant changes have been made, but the norm is not far from the stereotype.

Much of the learning in seminary is devoted to clarifying belief and to gaining the skills necessary to administer the local church. These are seen as ends in themselves.[8] Likewise, many "ministry schools" in local churches are concerned with imparting information and teaching skills needed to keep the church running, such as leading songs, teaching Sunday school and visitation. They do not fully engage the layperson with his or her specific calling both in the church and the world. As replicas of the seminary, how could they?

Practical theology is "the Cinderella of the seminary."[9] I say this with some uneasiness, for it is the discipline I occasionally teach. Karl Rahner, arguing for restoring practical theology to its true dignity, wants to rebuild the whole of theological education around the doing of theology. As Loren Mead has wryly commented, "You can't flunk out by lousing up the local congregation. You might foul up in Old Testament, but you can't flunk field ed."[10]

Surveying the seminary educational process from the perspective of an adult educator, V. S. T. Tyndale describes the seminary as a "filling station at which the student in three or four years is pumped full of a lifetime supply of ecclesiastical fuel."[11] He remarks that Jesus did not teach a course on the "Pharisees—origins, beliefs and practices." Jesus took the disciples into confrontation with the Pharisees and taught them "on the go." His approach was pragmatic.

Professional Thinking

Another negative consequence of professionalism—just as harmful as using professional training models for equipping in the church—is a professional mentality. A professional is one who claims a body of knowledge and a repertory of skills that are not shared by others. With these prerogatives, which the professional rigorously defends, it is easy for him or her to claim a monopoly on certain functions and services.

V. S. T. Tyndale has identified a number of factors that tend to promote the professionalism of the clergy:[12]

□ full-time work with full financial support

□ a quasi-unique function which has some social significance

□ increasing specialization

□ discouragement of amateurism with the assumption that one well-trained person can do it better

□ specialized functions seen as interchangeable and therefore capable of being performed by another professional (for instance, another pastor).

In contrast, Scripture teaches that financial support is a possibility but not inherent in the call to ministry (1 Cor 9:17); that no minister has a role which excludes the participation of others in the body from the functions, say, of teaching and sacramental ministry (Col 3:16); that, instead of increasing specialization, we should look forward to increasing diversification and fullness (Eph 4:7, 12); that acknowledging and honoring the contribution of the weaker and less appreciated brother is the heart of body unity (1 Cor 12:24-25); that no one is interchangeable, each ministry and each minister being a unique charism (gift) of God.

Professional thinking influences lay training in the local church in a variety of ways. Supported ministers may see their equipping task, for example, as one of delegation. A pastor may set up situations and courses to help other members of the church perform tasks (such as song leading or administration) *to assist him* in his unique ministry. Worse still, he may deliberately equip others to do those ministerial tasks which he does not think important or valuable, such as hospital visitation.

Supported ministers may set up training programs not for the lay ministry but for lay pastors. That is, a pastor may indoctrinate a few of his chosen members in the special privileges of the separated ministry on the assumption that some of these lay pastors will be able to be preachers in smaller country churches. He may hope that some of them will hear the call of God and go to seminary for full ministerial training.

There *is* a special role for the professional. But it is neither to move amateurs toward professionalism nor to train pastoral assistants. Rather supported ministers are to make themselves dispensable by giving away everything they have. As they do this, they will also need to be ministered to. After all, we cannot be our own minister, no matter how well trained we are. Their primary function—equipping the saints for ministry—is the one most calculated to deprofessionalize them.

Supported ministers, while agreeing that they have no special prerogatives in skills, may concentrate on imparting what their seminary education has given them an abundance of—information. Following the pattern of didactic seminary lectures, a pastor can set up his local church as a small-scale seminary. Sadly, there are always those who are all too ready to be initiated into the mysteries of theological language and the mythology of the clerical elite.

Supported ministers may set up a school within the church for the sole purpose of providing training for ministry in the church, the ecclesia. If the church has been commissioned to preach to the whole cosmos and to participate in the inbreaking of God's kingdom, then equipping must be *for life in the world*. It is precisely here that the seminary model fails us most poignantly. "Theology in its ultimate purpose," writes James Hopewells, "is meant to inform and transform the world. But in its existing seminaries we seem to use the world to inform and transform our theology."[13]

It is precisely at this point of involvement in the world that church members feel most helpless and most in need of equipping. Dorothy Sayers said that the average church member is "about as well equipped to do battle on fundamentals with a Marxian atheist or a Wellsian agnostic as a boy with a pea-shooter facing a fanfare of machine guns."[14]

The word *diaspora*—the church dispersed—may prove to be a useful companion to the word *ecclesia*—the church gathered. The Jews applied the word *diaspora* to their brethren whenever they were away from their homeland. In captivity in Babylon, in the Roman Empire and wherever they went, they did not lose their identity in spite of the hostile environment. They were still God's laity. Which is why Elton Trueblood was once heard to say that "church-goer is a vulgar, ignorant word; it must never be used; you are the church wherever you go."

Equipping then must equip the laity for dispersion, for witness and life in society, for what in the Roman Catholic Church came to be called the "lay apostolate." Having attempted to diagnose the problem, I now owe an equal attempt to designing an alternative.

Designing an Ecclesiastical Equipping Model

The starting point in securing an equipping structure in the local church is, strangely enough, to relinquish control of the church! If Jesus is really Head and if he is in touch with every member of the body, he can be counted on to be more interested in equipping than we are. That is a matter of profound spiritual relief. It is the basis of our equipping strategy.

Picture a large iceberg, nine-tenths of which is under water. Most ecclesiastical equipping is like that portion hidden from view: unless the structure and spirit of the church frustrate the work of God, the equipping generally takes place unnoticed, even unplanned. How else can we account for the seemingly spontaneous witness of the primitive church? There were no flip charts, no video presentations, no professional seminars. Yet "all the Jews and Greeks who lived in the province of Asia heard the word of the Lord" (Acts 19:10).

In a church structured and ordered in a New Testament way, people grow up in ministry through suffering, through life-centered learning experiences and disappointing ministry experiences, through regular and consistent Bible exposition, through exhortation, admonishment and modeling. Luther said once that it was by living and by dying, by being damned and by being saved that we become theologians, not by reasoning and speculating.

Much of this healing ministry and growth toward maturity is unplanned. Nevertheless, two structural features must be present for equipping to "happen" unintentionally. First, *structure must be participational rather than representative.* The professional ministry model says "let the one who does it best do it all the time." Let the best teacher teach; let the best worship leader lead. A participational structure creates opportunities for as many people as possible to participate.

Second, *structures must be relational rather than organizational.* That is, structures should be built around existing relationships and should serve those relationships rather than requiring the forming of relationships around and within the formal organization of the church. Rather than expecting all missions projects to originate always and only from the missions committee, for example, a church might create a support structure around a small group of people devoted to reaching teens.

Consider the iceberg once again. The one-tenth above water—intentional equipping—should resemble the nine-tenths underwater—unintentional equipping. The equipping we decide and intend to do ought to be characterized by participation rather than representation, by organic rather than organizational factors. The training *we* plan should take into consideration the ministries and gifts the Head is already prompting in his body. The difficulty or impossibility of doing this in a seminary context is another reason why that model is largely inadequate. The life of the local church is the arena of ministry development. To do this, two strategic factors must be considered: situational learning and structural flexibility.

Every educator knows that learning takes place best at the moment a question is asked. "When your son asks you . . ." (Deut 6:20) is the Old Testament model of family nurture. The whole of one's personal preparation is focused on that one question.

Jesus himself exemplified situational equipping: a careful analysis of his use of questions shows that while the modern educator asks five questions for every one question raised by the student, Jesus, as reported in the Gospels, had more questions asked of him than he asked. He constantly used situations to train the disciples. A. B. Bruce's monumental study *The Training of the Twelve* shows that Jesus' three-year training course covered every conceivable topic from fasting to divorce. But the learning usually took place at the disciple's initiative or in a situation of confrontation.

Aquila and Priscilla used Apollos's bad sermon as an opportunity to train Apollos more perfectly in the way of the Lord.

Recently, in our own fellowship, many people were asking for some guidelines on sexual behavior. Some had befriended homosexuals and were struggling to know how to relate. There was a lot of confusion about masculinity and femininity. It was a moment of readiness to learn.

The elders and staff of our church decided to minister to the situation by means of a symposium on sexuality. On Sunday we taught on sexuality from Scripture. Monday evening we gathered our small group leaders, our first-line pastoral workers, for a pastoral training session on handling sexual problems. We canceled our house groups that week, so that on Tuesday, Wednesday and Thursday we could offer seminars on various aspects of sexual behavior: "Is Dating Still the Best Way to Get Married?" "Lust and Love," "Sexual Healing," "Homosexuality," "To Bed or to Wed," "Is Living Together a Good Way to Prepare for Marriage?" Because we addressed an issue that was already agitating the body, the equipping impact was no doubt much greater than if we had decided for abstract reasons to introduce a program on sexuality as part of the educational curriculum of the church.

Three New Testament Models

To respond in this way to situations obviously requires *structural flexibility*. The New Testament offers three exciting models of equipping structures in the local church. I call them *the walking seminary, the open school in the marketplace* and *the advance-retreat pattern.*

The careful study of what Paul Benjamin calls "Paul's walking seminary" shows that the apostle Paul used his missionary journeys as opportunities for mobile equipping. Surrounding himself with those who could later replace him, he worked first with Barnabas (Acts 13:2), then with Silas (Acts 15:40). Such discipling relationships do not always succeed (see Acts 15:36-41). God's grace was manifest to Paul as he was blessed with new team partners. The "we" passages in Acts (beginning at 16:11) indicate that Dr. Luke had joined the walking seminary. Who knows how they must have discussed Scripture and the life and teachings of Jesus as they sailed to Samothrace and on to Philippi! Timothy was discovered in Lystra (16:3); he joined Silas and Paul. With their assistance in Corinth, Paul was apparently released to "devote himself exclusively to preaching" (18:5).

At Corinth Paul picked up the tentmaking couple Aquila and Priscilla (18:18), who were to become his ministry companions in three major cities. Erastus, mentioned as one of the helpers he picked up in Ephesus (19:22), was undoubtedly one of the men who accompanied Paul (17:15). Traveling once again into what is now northern Greece, Paul was "accompanied by Sopater son of Pyrrhus from Berea, Aristarchus and Secundus from Thessalonica, Gaius from Derbe, Timothy also, and from the province of Asia Tychicus and Trophimus" (20:4). Luke mentions their homes as though to make clear that Paul has representatives in this traveling, ministering and training group from most of the places where he has planted churches. He must have found potential leaders in each city and invited them to join him.

The Paul-Timothy relationship is often presented as the ideal equipping model. But who knows what influence Paul's peer Barnabas, or Dr. Luke himself, had on him? On at least one occasion, Luke and the others pleaded with Paul not to go to Jerusalem where he was sure to be in danger (21:12). But he was determined to go. Just as metal is forged and tempered by hammer and by heat, so these missionary teams learned and matured. Theology was incarnated as they laid down their lives for Christ and the gospel. This walking seminary will forever model the principle that the best way to train ministers is to send them on a mission of evangelizing and church planting—better still, *take* them.

This model is used with great success by Inter-Varsity Christian Fellowship and Youth with a Mission, just to mention two examples. But it is a model that can be incorporated into the local church to even greater advantage.

In our fellowship the staff elders developed a tentmaking internship model that involved training while working a job and ministering in a local church. In addition, they traveled as teams to minister in other centers and learned much through guided reflection.

One of Paul's longest missionary stays was at Ephesus where he taught in a rented public hall, the hall of Tyrannus. This is the prototype of the *open school in the marketplace*. In his classic study *Evangelism in the Early Church,* Michael Green called this "a most impressive piece of Christian opportunism."[15] That the Asiarchs—officials of the imperial cult—tried to prevent Paul from risking his life indicates clearly that his daily public teaching must have reached an otherwise "unchurched" clientele. This daily public teaching, later to be imitated by Origen's "lay" school in Alexandria, must have been effective in equipping the local Christians. For "all the Jews and Greeks who lived in the province of Asia heard the word of the Lord" (19:10) and this could not have resulted from Paul's teaching alone, but from those whom Paul instructed.

The Western text of Acts 19:9 adds that Paul taught daily for two years from eleven in the morning until four in the afternoon; these were the siesta hours. Paul must have redeemed this slack time by instituting Tyrannus's own lecture program for evangelism and lay training. F. F. Bruce aptly comments: "He must have infected his hearers with his own energy and zeal, so that they were willing to sacrifice their siesta for the sake of listening to Paul."[16]

Here "school" is given a fresh orientation: It is in the marketplace where the seeking non-Christian may join the believer in learning; learning takes place where *ecclesia* and *diaspora* meet. And it is a place of interaction. The word *dialegomenos* (19:9) suggests discussion, give and take, or what we call today discovery learning. Adults learn best (and are equipped best) when they can reflect on their own personal meanings and values in a nonthreatening environment. What the world really needs is not a good five-cent psychiatrist but what Carl Jung called a good school for forty-year-olds.[17]

Paul's school was also "open." People could come and go in a non-regimented manner, absorbing and applying at their own pace and level.

Nor could faith ever be treated in an abstract, theoretical way in this school. The presence of the non-Christians whom Paul earnestly desired to win for Christ, the presence of visitors who would return to the boondocks of Asia, the presence of Christian craftsmen losing their jobs because of the spread of Christianity demanded relevance. St. Francis left us with a saying that is deep and wise: "Man has as much knowledge as he executes."[18]

One practical application of this school-in-the-world idea has been our marriage enrichment ministry. Gail and I have offered this many times as a weekend package for believers at a retreat center. But last year we took our theory and practice seminars into the neighborhood by renting a local coffee house for four Friday evenings. Members of our fellowship could come for the teaching only if they brought some seeking neighbors. It was a first hesitant step toward an open school.

Mark's Gospel particularly shows an *advance-retreat pattern* in Jesus' ministry: the rhythm of the outstroke of activity and the backstroke of reflection. Each without the other is anemic. Together they embody Jesus' genius as a teacher. Jesus led the disciples into active, even aggressive ministry, retreated with them for reflection, evaluation and further instruction, then led them out again.

A learning structure in the local church is the use of retreats. On a retreat we move from our usual environment to a new environment, usually free of distractions, to gain perspective that will enable us to return to our usual environment with a renewed vision and purpose. Conferences and retreats have their greatest value when the *same people* share both the retreat and the advance—which explains the chief weakness of training seminars that are parachuted into our cities.

Some of the ways a local church can strategically use retreats for equipping are as follows:

□ a *congregational retreat* at the beginning of the year to focus priorities and build relationships

□ an *elders retreat,* to focus on individual vision and gifting of each elder, a matter usually crowded out of the agenda

□ a retreat focusing on *work and vocation*

□ a retreat on the *disciplines of the spiritual life,* to let people experience an extended period of silence and to learn new patterns of prayer and spiritual formation

□ a *house group retreat,* to provide an extended relaxed setting in which members can relate especially to family members not usually in the meeting

□ a *finance committee retreat,* to pray and to study biblical stewardship

□ a *mission committee retreat,* to interview prospective missionaries and to prayerfully develop a mission philosophy

□ a *marriage enrichment weekend,* to allow couples to have a sustained period without children in a relaxed setting to get them talking again

□ an *urban retreat,* to take advantage of the city—its needs, its resources and its subcommunities—to plunge people into new learning situations.

According to Howard Snyder, John Wesley understood many of these strategies and incorporated them into his ministry.

The experience of John Wesley shows what most Christians suspect: that the essential qualifications for effective, redemptive ministry have little if anything to do with formal education or ecclesiastical status and everything to do with spiritual growth, maturity and structural flexibility.

On the other hand, Wesley would not tolerate incompetence. He worked hard training his helpers and traveling preachers. He practiced theological education by extension two centuries before anyone thought up the name. Preachers carried books and pamphlets for themselves and for others. They were expected constantly to "improve the time" by up to six hours daily in study. In addition, Wesley seldom traveled alone: he often took one or more helpers with him so they could observe and learn from him.[19]

Snyder's study of Wesley as a model for radical Christianity today is a fitting reminder that we have the structure in place to train the nonprofessional. All we need to do is use it.

4. How to Build a Church around a Bus Stop

The phrase was a joke in our fellowship: "Marineview Chapel has become a bus stop disguised as a church." There was indeed a bus stop in front of the door. But the saying stopped being a joke when Graeme, one of our tentmaking elders, admitted that he was its author. For him it was a matter of great concern.

With a broken heart he confessed to the congregation that this is how he had come to feel about his little church that in a few years had mushroomed from one hundred to four hundred. He felt that people lined up each week for what they could get, just as people gather at a bus stop. The students used to say they had to go to bed early Saturday in order to rise early enough to get a seat at the 8:30 A.M. service. But we never knew whether the same people would be there next week at the same time—just like a bus stop.

There was no lack of warmth, no lack of God-honoring worship, no lack of sound teaching, no lack of mature leadership. It was a problem with the wineskin, not the wine. The problem was structural. And structures are important. Wineskins contain and preserve the wine. If this structure is not sound, two tragedies will occur when the wineskins burst: "the wine will run out" (Lk 5:37); the life of the kingdom of God will be wasted without being creatively given to the world. And "*both* the wine and the wineskins will be ruined*" (Mk 2:22); not only will the container be spoiled but even its contents.

Therefore equippers must be concerned about structures; they must deal with some very earthy factors: size, leadership, communication, flexibility. They cannot ignore the "human" factor because, as Howard Snyder says so wisely on this subject, "wineskins are the point of contact between the wine and the world. They are determined both by the wine's properties and the world's pressures. Wineskins result when the divine gospel touches human culture."[1]

In order to share with you what I have learned about structures that facilitate equipping, I must tell you a little about Marineview Chapel. We have a large and transient congregation. Many of our members are students and most people are under forty. All of our members—with the exception of core families who live near our building—seem to validate the census bureau claim that "Canadians move every four years." We were not anonymous masses gazing at one another's backs in a glittering

"We'll never get anywhere if you keep asking so many questions, Harry!"

edifice, while being entertained by a superstar. Nor could we be charged with a "goods and services" church mentality—marketing spiritual experiences on Sunday, after which people returned to their separate lives unconnected and possibly unconverted.

But we did have problems. Our little building seats one hundred twenty people comfortably, two hundred with standing room. And we were welcoming four hundred to five hundred each Sunday in two services. Core members were tired of reaching out to visitors only to find, in many cases, they never came back or went to a service at a different time. Relationships were becoming superficial, on Sunday at least. And the tentmaking elders were growing increasingly frustrated with the complexities of leading a large church—by Canadian standards.

With this biographical sketch of Marineview Chapel, remember the dimensions of church life we discovered in Ephesians 4: the church is more a monarchy than a hierarchy; the church must function as an organism rather than an organization; the church has servant leaders not leading servants; the church is moving toward a goal. What we as a body learned about equipping structures was forged on the anvil of these biblical principles by the hammer of the facts of life at Marineview Chapel. Each of these principles is a useful way to approach the question of appropriate structures.

Facilitating the Headship of Jesus

If the church is more a monarchy than a hierarchy, it is essential that every member of the fellowship be connected with the Head. The king speaks directly to his citizens, not through a ruling council. The elders' primary function is not to administer the headship of Jesus but to get each member into a personal responsive relationship with the living Christ.

This was already happening in an extensive way. First, we had developed a *house group structure* to facilitate fellowship and gift ministry. About seventy-five per cent of our church was active in small groups meeting weekly in homes. The groups had four purposes: study of the Bible, fellowship, worship and mission. The house group structure has proved ideal in drawing out the less aggressive person who might not participate openly on Sunday. Each person's gift had a natural opportunity to be discovered. Each person's faith could be nourished. Without doubt, small groups are the single greatest tool we have for developing spiritual gifts.

Second, we had structured the church with an emphasis on *individual and family growth* rather than Sunday services. Our concern was to get people and families into Christ. Using the structure of a house (figure 1), George Mallone developed a simple illustration of this while he was

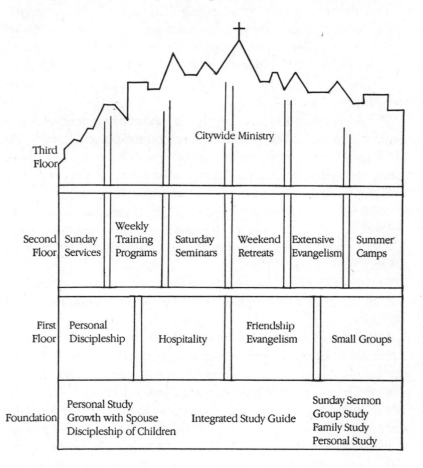

Figure 1. An Equipping Structure[2]

a teaching elder at Marineview Chapel.

The *foundation,* the most strategic part, is not the Sunday service. Rather, it is building people's personal lives in God. Growth cannot happen here without daily time in Bible reading and prayer. Just as important is the opportunity for accountability and sharing that our personal and family study guides encourage. Because we write these study guides ourselves, they are especially relevant for the kind of people *we* are.[3]

The first floor is built of interpersonal relationships and small groups. We encourage younger believers to meet with older believers. We try to keep the number of meetings at the Chapel to a minimum. We want people to have time for their families, time to talk over the back fence with a neighbor and time to pursue the Lord's special leading in the neighborhood or city.

The second floor is built of large groups and congregational events— Sunday services, Saturday seminars, weekend retreats and camps. This is the *third* level of priority because, as George Mallone observes, "major change in the church does not happen at the Sunday service level."[4]

The third floor is citywide ministry: interchurch worship and inspirational rallies, interchurch missions festivals, citywide demonstrations for social justice, and leadership training events and enterprises. These are the *product* of the lower levels of involvement and are built on them.

This strategy of decentralizing the church was one which the Lord had led us to embrace. It served to enhance the "monarchy model" of authority.

Occasional *special events* were a third structural member which we created in order to encourage personal relationship to Christ. From time to time we would design an event to creatively draw out further gifts "missed" by our normal life. For instance we celebrated a "gifts fair." We recruited about thirty people (and invited some volunteers) to share their personal ministry passions—everything from photography to administration and hospitality. A gift did not have to be on any list in Ephesians 4 or Romans 12. It just needed to be something they loved doing for God. When our gift fair arrived, people signed up strictly on the basis of interest. We were all surprised at what God was doing with people, and some people were strategically encouraged by others with similar interests.

In a church conceived as a monarchy, the equipper is primarily an *environmental engineer,* creating among the people of God an environment in which the Lord's voice may be heard. This is one of our highest callings.

Facilitating Body Life

But equippers need to be *relational engineers* as well. The second principle from Ephesians 4 is that the church functions as an organism rather than as an organization. Therefore, church leaders, equippers in particular, function also as "relational engineers." They facilitate relationships between members of the body and build structures to facilitate the ministries *already in the church,* rather than creating ministries and trying to find people to fill the slots.

Fortunately, I survived my first encounter with institutional church leadership. I was a summer intern working in a downtown church. At our first staff meeting, the burden came down on the summer staff; we would personally staff all the church programs. There were thirty-three activities or groups meeting each week. We were to keep them going! We had come to the inner city with a missionary vision and we were being asked to lubricate the squeaky wheels. We even had to turn the wheels ourselves most of the time.

There *are* some advantages in the church with a leadership structure that looks like a business enterprise—a descending hierarchy where authority is passed down from pastors to elders to deacons to committees to the congregation. For example, while only the pastor has the complete overview, there is usually a slot for every person. Also, since many church organizations are replicated, especially within a denomination, Christians can move to another city and fit into a new church almost like replaceable parts in a machine. Such a church structure is user-friendly. It is unquestionably more efficient—efficient, that is, in doing almost everything except equipping, the primary task of church leadership.

66   *LIBERATING THE LAITY* □

The womb-to-tomb church program with a group for every interest and a group for every age has its advantages too. Most people know where they fit (singles group, senior citizens and so on) and do not have to make the uncomfortable adjustment to an intergenerational house group. They start by going to an activity or program, or attending a meeting. Leadership needs are predictable too. But the result is something less than the church. It is an organization, not an organism.

Emil Brunner was referring to this in *The Misunderstanding of the Church,* where he made this observation: "During the whole course of its history, by reason of the fact that it was essentially a collective rather than a fellowship, the church has not only neglected to create a true brotherhood in Christ, but in many ways has positively hindered such a development."[5]

But what would be the structural characteristics of an organic church?

Appropriate scale. Its size and the size of its groupings would be small enough to encourage relationship but large enough to fulfill its corporate calling. Small groups work best with eight to fourteen members. "It is estimated," writes Stephen Neill, "that the church which received the two letters to the Thessalonians consisted of not more than fifty members."[6] Plymouth Brethren assemblies have prospered in the past with totally voluntary leadership. But the average size of their assemblies is under a hundred. We were a church of four hundred, meeting in two services, trying to function with relational integrity. It wasn't working.

Simplicity. The house group is the essence of simplicity. It needs no president, vice president or nominating committee. Planning takes place as all the members talk together as a family. It is one living cell in the body of Christ.

Ownership. Instead of analyzing needs, planning, recruiting staff and accomplishing goals, church leaders can relax in the leadership of Jesus. He knows what is needed and he is in touch with every member, supplying gifts, vision and what used to be called "a burden." When people feel they "own" a ministry or mission, they do not need to be motivated.

Assuming that everyone is listening to the Lord, the mix of gifts and vision in the body at any given moment is clearly the Lord's agenda for that local church. There is nothing intrinsically wrong with starting with needs. But if we start with people—and their gifts and visions—the actions and programs which follow are more likely to be owned by the people than if we start with needs which "must" be met (by some unnamed person).

Peter and Monica came to me a few months ago with their vision. They felt that God might be calling them to a ministry of intercessory prayer. They wanted to start a house group with this particular focus. There was no existing slot in our church program for what they wanted to do. (I might have wished they would volunteer to teach Sunday school!) We challenged them to pray about their call and to see if any others wished to join them in this ministry. And this is just what has happened. It all came about more naturally than if the elders had tried to create an intercession group. Peter and Monica feel they "own" that ministry. It is theirs under the Lord.

A healing group started the same way. But imagine the more typical situation of some sister or brother complaining to the elders: "Why is there no group in the church that prays regularly for healing?" To the elders this usually translates to, "You leaders should do something about it!" There is no equipping of the saints in that.

But a door for equipping the saints is opened if the elders were to respond, "Is God saying something to *you* about the need to pray for healing? Why don't you ask him whether there is something he wants *you* to do? You seem to have seen a need the rest of us have missed. We'll pray for you as you try to find out if this is a genuine call of God. And we'll be glad to make it known to others who might join you in that. Keep in touch with us because we can direct you to some important resources in the area of healing."

It's risky, because letting people own their vision and ministry will lead some to fall flat on their faces. The leadership must be aware of this and be prepared to encourage people to learn through failure as well as success. It is a part of the equipper's calling to pick up pieces. There will be failures and short-lived projects. This leads to another principle of organic structure.

Flexibility. There are two reasons to defend flexibility besides the fact that it is a mark of a living organism. First, flexibility is necessary to accommodate individual persons. Second, flexibility is needed to be truly open to the Spirit's leading. Why, for example, should it be a tragedy for a house group to die? It might be a creative moment for every member, especially if the group ends with celebration, thanksgiving and sharing of what was learned.

Individual differences. This is not mere psychological jargon but a crucial factor in equipping. People *are* different. Rather than fitting people into structures, we will need to build appropriate structures around the people we have.

Flexibility is needed to remain open to fresh leading from the Holy Spirit. God wishes to surprise us and he cannot surprise us if we have already predicted structurally how God must enter our fellowship. To demand that God not interrupt us is to make an idol of him. We will then become as rigid and predictable as the image of God we worship: "Our God is in heaven; he does whatever pleases him. But their idols are . . . made by the hands of men. They have mouths, but cannot speak. . . . They have hands, but cannot feel. . . . *Those who make them will be like them, and so will all who trust in them*" (Ps 115:3-8).

For this reason our public gatherings of the church must be a balance of order and freedom, leadership and participation. It is unthinkable that those responsible for leading worship would give no forethought to the components they would wish to have in the service. But it is equally unthinkable that we would leave no room for spontaneity, for the Spirit's interruption. It may come through the weakest and most awkward member of the body.

In our pilgrimage we were trying to discover a solution to the busstop problem. We had looked at several alternatives: renting a large facility; building a large facility (the cost would be astronomical and we would not be able to keep fifty per cent of our budget for missions); sending a nucleus of believers to start a new work on the campus or in a restaurant somewhere; sending as many people as possible to assist a smaller church (easier said than done!); dividing our one congregation into three subcongregations, each sharing the building and the church's resources; starting a third service in our present building—two morning shows and one matinee in the afternoon!

But what we had not done was to lay down our agenda before our creative Lord and let him tell us what he wanted. So with careful preparation and some guidance by the elders, we called a day of repentance and prayer for the whole church. What happened that day was the beginning of our solution. It was more than simple modeling by the leaders of what the headship of Jesus means. The elders themselves needed to be ministered to. One after another of us was led into deep repentance for our superficial relationships. An elder confessed that he hardly ever prayed regularly and by name for each of the other elders. He spoke for the rest. His openness encouraged others to admit that the problem was deeper than structure, more subtle than mere numbers. The demon was in us.

As we wept together and rejoiced together that day, we stopped being a bus stop. But that was not the end of our problems for there was more than one structural issue yet to be resolved.

Facilitating Shared Leadership

Equipping happens best where the church has servant leaders and not leading servants. It is a nice distinction.

In practice it means that the leadership is thoroughly pastoral—nurturing people in the Lord—and thoroughly shared. Implied is a particular view of the authority leaders have. I heard Earl Palmer once describe it this way: "Where farms are small you need a lot of fences. But in Texas where the ranches are huge you hardly need any fences at all." And if we have a big God, we won't be afraid to share leadership. Therefore a fellowship which takes seriously that "we have one leader— Jesus" will not allow anyone, man or woman, to become the titular head of the church. That fences leadership in too tightly.

Early leaders of the Brethren movement were concerned that the public ministry should be shared for the health of the church. But, as the following conversation affirms, they were not simply advocating "the world's greatest amateur hour" with everyone who wanted to speak being given a turn. Wigram, an early Brethren leader, was asked, "Do you admit 'a regular ministry'?"

To this he replied, "If by a regular ministry you mean a *stated* ministry (that is, that in every assembly those who are gifted of God to speak for edification will be both limited in number and known to the rest), I do admit it; but if by a regular ministry you mean an *exclusive* ministry, I dissent."[7]

But the process of developing shared leadership while recognizing "stated" gifts and ministries is a delicate one indeed. In *Furnace of Renewal,* George Mallone gives an excellent summary of the scriptural reasons for eldership and the process of appointing new elders—on the basis of who is already serving as an elder.[8] With sensitive and extended teaching, these appointments can be made even in the context of democratic rule.

But the real challenge of plural eldership is in those matters about which the Scripture says almost nothing. How many elders should you have? In the absence of an apostle like Paul, Timothy or Titus, how are they appointed? How are they to make decisions—by consensus, or by unanimity reached by prayer and fasting? What are they to do when they do not reach unity? What are the limits of their responsibility? And finally (the issue that concerned us in our bus-stop investigation), what are the elders to do when the body does not wish to follow their lead?

After weeks of prayer and discussion, the elders believed that one option seemed to best fulfill the Lord's mandate for Marineview. It was to divide the church into three congregations—we call them communities—each with its own cluster of elders, its own network of house groups, its own Sunday service and Sunday school. The elders believed that they should be the first to go the way of the cross. So they went through the agonizing process of deciding which elder would go where. They then convened a meeting of all our house leaders—about a quarter of the whole church—and presented the proposal, including times of meeting. And the house leaders wouldn't do it!

Here lies the nice distinction between servant leaders and leading servants. Servant leaders must always be open to a prophetic word, even a correction, from the body. Indeed a spiritual eldership is in part created by a spiritual body. So, licking their wounds, the elders went back to pray and listen once more. They did not intend to give up their vision.

But neither did they intend to foist their vision on the body *in the particular form* it had taken shape in their minds.

It was on the third meeting that the body and the elders became united on the *how* of the creation of three communities. It took a lot of time but, in its final form, the decision has been blessed by God. And the process of getting there was a crucial equipping moment in the congregation's history.

Facilitating the Church's Destiny

The church is moving toward a goal. It is a much richer goal than church growth measured by numbers. It is the full measure of Christ (Eph 4:13). Just as each Christian is a fraction of the image of Christ, so is each church. Therefore, while all local churches have the same final destiny of mature humanity in Christ, they will experience a unique sense of participation in that final destiny. I recount Marineview's journey not because it can be or should be reproduced, but because it is unique. Just as the journey of every other local church will be unique.

As we discerned the shape of our church's growth, we believed that Christ had led us to a few strong convictions. It was these that shaped our final decision, these which determined how we should equip the church. In other words, once we had determined how God had equipped us, we needed to find the appropriate structures to equip ourselves.

We were convinced of *the normalcy of tentmaking leadership.* The tentmaking elders had become frustrated and weary with a large and unwieldy congregation. While we *could* have grown larger—perhaps up to a thousand—we would have done so only by increasing the level and importance of the professional staff team.

We were convinced that *the church exists in part to equip all its members for ministry.* That isn't its only reason to exist—perhaps it is not even its primary purpose—but it is one implication of being the body of Christ. Participation, ownership, proximity, experimentation are all essential to this. We therefore judged that by dividing into three communities we would *multiply* the need for leadership and service of all kinds and thereby create an equipping structure.

We were convinced that *the quality of the church's life was measured not by its activity but by the depth of its community.* A community is an environment and, as Stephen Clark has so carefully shown, it is the environment, more than teaching, that changes people.

If the church was to be an environment of love and mutual support, several factors had to intersect. The same people needed to keep seeing each other. The group had to have some *stability.* It had to be small enough for people to know and be known. People had to intersect in a variety of relationships—worship, fellowship, planning, recreation, work. To do this we had to stop being a church with multiple services and become three communities that formed one church. We could celebrate our unity by occasional combined services and through shared resources. But the bottom line would be the community.

We were convinced that *the particular way Marineview was called to grow into Christ was by reproducing.* We had already started one new church in suburban Vancouver. We did not have the natural nucleus to start another. But our commitment to three communities was an active step toward readiness to start a new church. It was a strategic step to train church-planting leadership.

The old fable about the tortoise and the hare is a counterbalance to a chapter on structure. The hare had the right structure but he wasn't motivated to win—or perhaps he was just self-confident. The tortoise had the wrong structure for a race—it was inflexible, visible and impenetrable—like the structure of many churches. But he won anyway.

There is a delicate interplay between structure and Spirit. We cannot make spiritual renewal happen by having the right structures. But by clinging to the wrong structures we *can* prevent some renewal—and some ministry development—from ever happening.

Facilitating Structural Change

How can structures be changed? It helps if the church is desperate. Failing desperation, a revival is the next best hope for change. But neither of these can be orchestrated. But some progress can be made by equipping leaders who wish to implement some needed structural change. In order to illustrate and for the sake of clarity, let us imagine that the hoped-for structural change is the introduction of small groups to a church that does not yet have them.

Pray for the change. If it isn't from God and if your own heart is not right, you are better off to stick with a Spirit-filled tortoise.

Teach for one year *before* you hope something will happen. Your teaching will need to focus on various relational and ministry needs that cannot be met in the existing structures.

Proclaim the biblical precedent and biblical foundation for the proposed change. For example, the phrase "church in their house" in Paul's letters shows that the house church rather than the sanctuary church was the New Testament norm. We need both today, but for different needs.

Find historical parallels. For instance, Luther *would have* instituted house groups if he could have found some people who wanted them.

The third kind of service should be a truly evangelical order and should not be held in a public place for all sorts of people. But those who want to be Christians in earnest and who profess the gospel with hand and mouth should sign their names and meet alone in a house somewhere to pray, to read, to baptize, to receive the sacrament, and to do other Christian works.

According to this order, those who do not lead Christian lives could be known, reproved, corrected, cast out, or excommunicated, according to the rule of Christ, Matthew 18:15-17. Here one could also solicit benevolent gifts to be willingly given and distributed to the poor. Here would be no need of much and elaborate singing. Here one could set up a brief and neat order for baptism and the sacrament and center everything on the Word, prayer, and love.

In short, if one had the kind of people and persons who wanted to be Christians in earnest, the rules and regulations would soon be ready. But as yet I neither can nor desire to begin such a congregation or assembly or to make rules for it. For I have not yet the people or persons for it, nor do I see many who want it.[9]

Invite people to try bite-sized chunks. Without destroying the Wednesday-night prayer meeting, the congregation can be invited to a six-week series in various homes using the same study guide. Some people will get so "hooked" on real fellowship that you may never get them back!

Demonstrate the truth you wish to convey. I have been in a small group for each of the twenty-eight years that I have followed Christ. That fact says more about my view of the importance of small groups than I ever could verbally.

Allow people to move into new structures—wherever possible—*at their own pace.* Many churches find that continuing a Wednesday prayer meeting or midweek meeting is essential for those unready for house groups.

If all else fails, *pray for a change of spiritual climate in the church.* Standing in the London Museum, a tourist was looking at the skeleton of a huge dinosaur. It was not the impressive structure that captured his interest though. "Whatever happened to the dinosaur? Why did the dinosaur die out?" Very simply the answer came: the climate changed.

No structure will last forever. And perhaps the hare won't take advantage of his better structure anyway! And we must not forget that we are always in danger of becoming once again "a bus stop disguised as a church."

Part III
Theology for Equipping the Laity

5. The Ministry of Work

Joseph is the Old Testament prototype of the Christian equipped for work. Like us, he found it difficult to be in the world without being of it. He is an example of both how to live completely and Christianly in the world, and how *not* to.

After interpreting Pharaoh's dreams, he emerged from prison and was soon administering a program of food and economic control in Egypt. He was overseer of Egypt as a saint in *diaspora*.

The focus of Part 2 was structures for equipping in the church as *ecclesia*—the work of ministry. In Part 3 I will analyze the equipping necessary to prepare the church for its *diaspora* role—the ministry of work. The trick is to hold these two together, as Joseph's story will illustrate.

Toward the end of the story, Joseph had acquired a completely Egyptian identity. God had raised him from prison to palace to become

Pharaoh's deputy prime minister to save the nation in the famine years. But his identity had become thoroughly attached to his work and his adopted culture. Pharaoh gave him an Egyptian name, Zaphenath-Paneah, and an Egyptian wife, Asenath, the daughter of a priest, which had implications for his religious life. Significantly, Joseph gave his first son the Egyptian name Manasseh which sounds like the Hebrew word for "forget." As Joseph explained it, "God has made me forget all my trouble and *all my father's household*" (Gen 41:51). Was this a grateful forgetting of the injury? or a deliberate forgetting of the inheritance? Did Joseph want to lose his identity as part of the family of promise?

Joseph had a lot to forget and even more to forgive. His father had pampered him as the favorite son (Gen 37:3); his brothers hated him and conspired to eliminate him (37:4, 18); they sold him to some traders who took him to Egypt as a slave (37:28; 39:1); in Egypt his master's wife, after trying unsuccessfully to seduce him, framed him and had him put in prison (39:11-12, 20).

When he was finally released from prison, Joseph became the perfect layman fully equipped to live in this world for God. But he was also a believer living a double life, as his relationship with his brothers clearly shows.

His passionate self-revelation, "I am Joseph" (45:3), signaled the end of the dichotomy in his own identity. At the same time it can be regarded as his greatest expression of his faith.

When his brothers came to him for grain, not knowing that the Egyptian ruler was their own kin, Joseph did not make himself known. He played with them, now kind, now harsh, like sunshine and frost, to break up the hard soil of their hearts. They needed to be brought to a full recognition of what they had done to Joseph. Therefore, Simeon was bound before him; one of the brothers was ransomed for the rest; Benjamin was treated as a favorite brother at the feast. And perhaps these contrived experiences were the God-appointed means for Joseph to come to terms with his bitterness against his family. They reflect the struggle going on inside him.

Months later he reveals himself in what has been called the greatest recognition scene in all literature. But more significantly than the dramatic impact was the spiritual breakthrough. His declaration, "I am Joseph," was the end of his personal dichotomy. He was not only an Egyptian and a ruler. He was also a member of God's family. He was not only a saint in *diaspora* but a saint in *ecclesia.*

Equipping for Career Choices

Like most moderns Joseph had three careers in his lifetime. He was a shepherd in Canaan, a slave in Potiphar's house, and an administrator in Egypt. In each his work was a ministry.

It could be said that he had a career, a job and a vocation, in that order. Being a shepherd was a *career* because, as Webster defines it, a career is "a profession or occupation which one trains for and pursues *as a life work.*" Joseph undoubtedly expected to be a shepherd for life, in spite of his dreams. Being a *slave* and then a prisoner was *a job.* Joseph experiences work as drudgery in spite of his natural ability to take over every situation in which he found himself. Being Pharaoh's prime minister was a *vocation* because in this capacity Joseph *saved* Egypt and Israel. As Webster defines it, a vocation is "a call, a summons or an impulsion to perform a certain function or a certain career, *especially a religious one.*" Joseph was called to save his own family and his neighbors through his so-called secular work, in spite of the fact that he was unaware of this call of God until later (Gen 45:5, 7-8; 50:19-20).

But not one of the three did he choose. They were chosen for him. Precisely this fact makes Joseph a good model to keep before us as we equip people for career choices. A sense of the sovereignty of God is the necessary support for those feeling the crushing burden of career choices.

God's sovereignty over all of life means, first, that *your life is divinely ordained and significant.* You are not an accident. The way you are put together is part of God's design for your involvement in the world. In *The Eighth Day of Creation,* Elizabeth O'Connor tells how God has written his will for you into your very being. Quite literally, your gifts are you. Uncovering your gifts and essential motivations thus becomes one of your most important tasks. In light of the sovereignty of God, fulfilling your vocation is doing what comes naturally to you, whether speaking, writing, potting, sculpturing or administering.

The Sima test can help people get in touch with their basic motivational thrusts.[1] But there is a problem with discerning our vocation by discerning our "natures," as the Sima test itself inadvertently exposes. It lists "mother" as an inappropriate occupation for at least one personality type and "housewife" as a vocational disaster for two others. This is cold comfort for some mothers reading the book. And it would have been cold comfort indeed for Joseph in Pharaoh's prison, a position he did not choose and for which he was naturally unsuited.

Second, this sovereignty means that *there are many things you can do for God's glory, not just one.* Joseph was a shepherd, a slave and a savior, and God was with him in all three. He was a natural administrator but was called to move beyond what was natural to him. It is good to discern the sovereignty of God in our makeup and background. It is better to live for God in the foreground wherever we find ourselves. There is growth in that and grace.

It is not natural, for instance, for me to be an equipper. It is more natural for me to be a solo performer or even to create an equipping program. There are people who, in one sense, find equipping more congenial to their personalities. They are delighted to be a facilitator rather than a doer. They take great pleasure in seeing members of their team become fulfilled in ministry. Yet they too are called to move beyond the natural and to function not merely by who they are but by who they are *in Christ.*

Understanding the sovereignty of God is part of the answer for the person who feels vocationally dissatisfied and who, in the words of an underemployed but educated tool salesman, is holding a grudge against God "for withholding . . . the gift of appropriate employment."[2] There is more than one thing you can do to perform God's will. God does not have a wonderful *plan* for your life. He has something far better: a wonderful *purpose.*

Third, as Joseph saw, *the only real mistake you can make is to not want to do God's will, not want to glorify God where you are.* There are no other vocational "mistakes," not even in the choice of a marriage partner, because our sovereign, loving God takes everything we do and weaves it into his own purpose.

Handmade Persian carpets are full of mistakes. But the carpets turn out beautifully because when the master weaver sees a mistake in the weaving, with his helpers along each side, he incorporates the mistake into his now-altered design. Our sovereign God never makes a mistake, never fails.

Fourth, *the very worst that can happen to you in your career can turn out to be God's training for something more.* We are equipped for the kingdom in the furnace of life. It was no accident that Joseph was thrown down the pit; he was an informer and an opinionated prig (Gen 37:2, 5-11). Being put in Pharaoh's prison was the appointed means of getting him into Pharaoh's court. Ministry came out of work, not work out of ministry (a matter to be developed in the next chapter). God prepares us for kingdom work by what we learn in so-called secular work.

Fifth, *in whatever job, career or vocation you find yourself, you are called to walk by faith rather than by sight.* Joseph could not find the meaning of his life by looking at the fruit of his labor. The meaning of his life was found in his relationship to God. Like Joseph, you may not know how God led you, how God used you until long after. Perhaps not even in this life will you be able to say, "It was not you who sent me here, but God" (Gen 45:8).

Equipping to Relate Work and Ministry

For a time I combined work in our construction business (I had bought into the company by this time) with part-time remunerated work in the ministry of the church. I have more than a little empathy for the person who is attempting to find the right balance of work and ministry. It is a matter of discernment not only of your own person and the particular church in which you serve but also of where you are in your own pilgrimage.

One day during this period, I looked back over one week's activities. I had spent some quality time with one of my children. Gail and I had our weekly "date" in the library and lunch out; we had lots to talk about. (I regard being a husband and father as my highest priority in the kingdom.) I also did some bookkeeping for the company to resolve a discrepancy in the bank's records. In the course of that I had a long session with the bank manager. I also typed some invoices. During these same days, I studied a passage of the Bible intensively in preparation for a sermon. I counseled, pushed paper in the church office and attended some meetings. On Sunday I "labored," as Paul called it, at preaching.

It was all work and it was all ministry. Each part of the week was part of my kingdom vocation: family, church, work and society. I am hard pressed to defend one part of my week as more sacred than another. Whether work or ministry comes first is obviously a complex question. It is much simpler if you say that ministry in the church is more important than ministry in the world. Then, if you are a serious Christian, you simply try to get into the ministry and do it all the time. But the Bible will not let me off that easily.

Discerning the Choices

There are three ways today to relate work and ministry. The professional Christian, the Christian professional and the tentmaker. Professional Christians are fully supported Christian workers—whether a pastor, a youth minister, a leader in parachurch work or a missionary—whose ministry is their work and whose work is their ministry.

Christian professionals sense the call of God to a very demanding career, such as medicine, politics or education. I believe that someone called to homemaking during the younger years of his or her children has a similarly demanding holy vocation. Earlier I mentioned that Gibbs and Morton called such a person, whose interest is primarily in the world outside the church building, a layperson type A. It is usually not possible for such professionals to engage heavily in a ministry that does not relate directly to their work. In this case, work is the primary arena of ministry and ministry comes out of work. Joseph as prime minister of Egypt is the classic example of this.

Aquila and Priscilla (Acts 18:1-4) as well as Paul are the biblical models of the tentmaker. Occasionally, Paul was supported by churches. But at Corinth he joined Aquila and Priscilla, making and selling tents to the Jewish refugees in the western Mediterranean.

© Leadership, 1984. Concept — Rodney Clapp. Artist — Nick Hobart.

"Yes, it's quite a nest, but they only use it once a week."

This slippery term *tentmaking* is best defined as the path of those who are called to a specific ministry, either in the church or the world, that is unrelated to the job or work by which they maintain themselves. Work supports ministry in this case. Gibbs and Morton's layperson B is the type of tentmaker whose interest in *ecclesia* ministry makes them look like voluntary clergy, as Roland Allen called this option.[3] Sometimes tentmakers will deliberately choose a less fulfilling and less demanding job to release time and energy for ministry.

I had just finished explaining this to a young man in a restaurant when an older man in the next booth, obviously eavesdropping, exclaimed, "That's me!" When I invited him to join us, we discovered that, though he was well educated, he was, by choice, a lift-truck operator. He had an extensive youth ministry and this job suited his ministry best. Sometimes a professional Christian can do the same thing. The early church must have been far richer in tentmakers than we are.

My first disturbing exposure to a tentmaking model was through a visiting pediatric specialist in Montreal. Dr. Salama was highly skilled in his field and was sought for teaching assignments in various hospitals and medical schools in North America. He accepted many invitations that required travel because, like Paul, he used his travel to propagate the gospel.

As a Spirit-filled Coptic Christian, he landed in Montreal with one overriding agenda—to locate and evangelize as many nominal Coptic Christians as he could find. He had eight weeks to do it. Just as Paul did when he arrived at Philippi (Acts 16:13), Dr. Salama went where he would most likely find people at prayer. During his eight weeks in Montreal, he tracked down Egyptians with any interest in their church background, invited them to his hotel and systematically explained the way of Christ to them. By the end of his tentmaking assignment in Montreal, he was scurrying around to find a continuing support structure for several new Christians. As it happened, I became part of that support system and, along with my partner John Hardy, nourished that group for a year until they became the nucleus of a new church.

I have no doubt that Dr. Salama had done the same thing in two or three other cities during that year. Would he have been more successful if he had been a paid mission agent to Copts in Montreal?

Making this choice between various work and ministry combinations is not an easy one. In my opinion, it is not a once-in-a-lifetime decision; we are repeatedly faced with these choices. Therefore God gives us the support, wisdom and counsel of those close to us in the local church to help us discern the best combination for ourselves at each stage of life.

Understanding the Choices

If you are "saved" only by the skin of your teeth and not very serious about the Christian life, you may attend church, but you will give yourself mainly to family, work and making money. Or you could be "just a homemaker." If you are more serious, you will choose a people-helping profession such as medicine, teaching or social work. But if you are really called, you will go into *the ministry,* a term invariably used to describe financially remunerated ministry in the church.

So runs a certain popular and pernicious train of thought in the church. As if being a homemaker were an unimportant task and as if all were not called to ministry.

But if some are called in a special way to the ministry and others are not, why does the Bible not clearly indicate this possibility? Why is "calling" never used in the plural? Why do the apostles speak of one calling, however diverse the spiritual gifts with which the believers are equipped? If we are to choose a combination of work and ministry, we must understand what the Bible teaches about our call to ministry and work.

First, there is no hierarchy of values in ministry. God ordains a Joseph to serve him as a shepherd, a slave and a savior. He ordained a woman, Mary, to bear his own Son into the human family. The supported, remunerated Christian worker is not more called to ministry than is the tentmaker or the Christian professional. They are all called.

Luther attacked this special call in his essay *On Monastic Vows:* "Monastic vows rest on the false assumption that there is a special calling, *a vocation,* to which superior Christians are invited to observe the counsels of perfection while ordinary Christians fulfill only the commands; but there is simply no special religious vocation since the call of God comes to each at the common tasks."[4]

Second, *diaspora* ministers (those called to express their primary ministry in society) are no less called to ministry than *ecclesia* ministers and have an equal need for training. Thankfully there are Christian training institutions (Regent College, New College Berkeley, The Institute for Christian Studies and others) designed to prepare believers to think Christianly about involvement in society for God.

That the professional equippers—the pastor, parish clergy and seminary professors—are unprepared to train people for their ministry on Monday is precisely stated by William Diehl.

In my opinion, our seminaries are . . . so victimized by their own academic institutionalism that not only are they failing to prepare the clergy for their role of equipping, but they are also supporting a philosophy which depreciates a theology of the laity. . . . Thus, the theologians inadvertently define what a church institution really is—an inward focusing principality which sustains its own life by directing all wisdom and training to those who have committed their lives in professional service to it.[5]

Today the alabaster jar of theological education needs to be broken and its contents spread not just in the church but in the world. The best place to train *diaspora* ministers, as we have already seen, is in the local church.

Third, there is no call directly from God to be financially supported in ministry. There is a call to ministry that comes to every believer. But the call to be supported comes from the church rather than from God. Paul spoke of support as a privilege and a right (1 Cor 9:4-23). But it is not a right to be pressed by the Christian worker, any more than a husband has the right to demand the submission of his wife or a wife of her husband.

Christian workers are free to accept the gifts of believers who wish to release them from certain kinds of toil for the sake of the ministry. But even when this support is offered, as it was with Paul, believers must discern whether it is in the best interests of the kingdom, or whether the gospel would be hindered (1 Cor 9:12).

In my opinion, Christian workers should not seek their own financial support when they feel called into full-time ministry. To write begging, manipulative letters to raise financial support is a misuse of ministry gifts.

I have just received another letter from a friend who wants desperately to be sent to the mission field. He spent a whole year tramping around the country raising his future monthly income. Each month's letter showed the thermometer a little higher. Finally, when he had raised twenty thousand dollars a year, his board asked him to raise an additional ten thousand for moving expenses. This young couple has been victimized by a system that is scripturally wrong and needs to be equipped. It is a structure "out of joint," dislocated, that needs to be set in place.

When those called to ministry are not voluntarily supported by those around them, they have a very clear scriptural mandate: work. Paul worked "night and day" to support his ministry (2 Thess 3:8). I am not disparaging the supported ministry (after all, currently I am a supported minister), but I do think we need to re-evaluate our support structures in light of biblical precedents.

Equipping to Resist the Temptations of Work

Joseph's life work—shepherd and slave, as well as savior—was a gracious divine discipline to guide him to God. The ministry of work rather than the work of the ministry was the arena in which he learned the meaning of Augustine's famous mot: "Thou, God, hast made us for thyself and our hearts are restless until they rest in thee."

In North America we are tempted to seek rest by escaping from work. We sell our time to an employer in exchange for money, with which we buy experiences to enjoy during our leisure hours. We have sanctioned a secular understanding of sabbath; the sabbath has now become the goal of work. Consequently, there is a deeper need for rest than the Sabbath principle can meet. We must learn to equip believers to find *rest in work.*

The whole design of creation in Genesis 1 and 2 focuses on the rest of God. Karl Barth reminds us that "the first conscious awakening of man in creation (because he was created in the evening of the sixth day) was to awake to the reality of the seventh day and to discover that God had already done everything."[6] Therefore rest is not simply a cessation from labor but, as Richard Baxter has suggested, an anticipation of what it will be like for heaven to be on earth.[7]

Augustine said this long before when he noted that the observance of the sabbath is not merely the setting aside of one day. Rather, "he who does whatever good work he does in the hope of future rest is already observing the everlasting sabbath in that grace."[8] In God, rest and work are not opposed. Therefore, Augustine, in expounding the creative role of Wisdom (the Son of God) in Proverbs 8:27-31, shows that God's work is like child's play.

From the story of Joseph, we may discern the three secret sources of the restlessness we experience when we seek rest apart from God.

The first source is the temptation to be the architect of our own fulfillment. Joseph was a shepherd with a dream of greatness (Gen 37:2). Whether these dreams were the projection of his own subconscious ambition to be better than his brothers or were God-inspired, we don't know. We can say this: Joseph had a high opinion of himself that came from God. That was unquestionably a good thing.

Not so good was what Joseph did when he attempted to implement his dreams—tattling on his brothers to put them down before his father and indiscreetly sharing the second dream. He should have kept the dream to himself and let God fulfill it in his own time and way.

Daniel Yankelovitch argues that what has changed today is not our willingness to work but what we want out of a job or career.[9] There are a whole new set of psychological satisfactions that are sought from jobs: it must be meaningful and interesting work, appropriate to our talents; it must lead to self-development and there must be a continuing challenge and discovery.

My grandfather Brown, on my mother's side, owned a schooner and sailed twice a year from Newfoundland to Labrador to fish for cod. After six to eight weeks, he returned with the hold burdened with salt cod. He did not work to express his personality. He worked to live. I have never been able to find out whether he liked fishing or sailing.

Grandmother Brown worked too, raising twelve children in a Newfoundland outport, spinning and weaving, knitting, putting up provisions for the winter months, hoeing the potatoes and serving up, day in and day out, that wonderful Newfoundland dish—fish and brews. In summer they augmented their diet with cabbage and potatoes. When an iceberg floated into Hare Bay, they would paddle out in a skiff, cut off some ice and make ice cream. Grandmother Brown worked to survive.

My father was the first in the family to break with work as a necessity. One day, while delivering bread with a horse-drawn carriage, he decided that he would not spend the rest of his life as his father had, as a baker. So he took accounting by correspondence and eventually became the president of a midsized steel fabrication company. He had a dream.

But it is what we do with our dreams that matters. It is *how* we work, rather than at what. We may be tempted to become, through work, the architect of our own fulfillment. The workaholic tries to find his fulfillment in work rather than in God. Caught by the idolatry of work, he is therefore deeply restless.

A second source of restlessness is the temptation to compromise righteousness for the sake of security. This happened while Joseph was a slave in Potiphar's house. Mrs. Potiphar attempted to seduce Joseph. One of the many dimensions to the temptation was the desire for security and power. An intrigue with an important Egyptian might lead to the fulfillment of his dream. In the same way, people are tempted to advance themselves at someone else's expense and to yield to baser desires to keep one's job.

Joseph successfully resisted the temptation and ended up in prison. But he would have been a lot more restless if he had compromised his righteousness to keep his job. "The LORD was with him" (Gen 39:21). The Lord can be trusted with any results that stem from our unconditional commitment to live righteously in the secular work world. Joseph was a stunning Old Testament example of the truth of Jesus' words: "Seek first his kingdom and his righteousness, and all these things will be given to you as well" (Mt 6:33).

A third source of restlessness is the temptation to attach one's identity to one's work. We have already seen how Joseph, now a savior, came to have a completely Egyptian identity. His identity was rooted in his job. It is just as easy for modern Christians to become identified with what they *do*, either as a ministry in the church or as a ministry in society. William Diehl exposes this deception:

> Without any doubt, the biggest gap between our confessed theology of Sunday and our operational theology of the week is that of works righteousness. On Sunday, we say we believe that God's grace alone has made us a whole and accepted person. On Monday, our actions betray a belief that our identity and worth are based entirely on what we do and how well we do it.[10]

God graciously challenges this dichotomy by sovereignly bringing into our lives brothers and sisters in God's family who challenge us. "I am Joseph" not only signaled Joseph's repentance from being isolated from the family of God; it was also his positive commitment of faith to throw in his lot with the poor, despised and suffering family of God and to let Zaphenath-Paneah and Joseph be one and the same person: man in *diaspora,* man in *ecclesia.*

Working for God, then, is not finding the perfect job and doing it heartily, as good a thing as that is. Working for God is trusting God to fulfill our dreams, trusting God to meet our needs if we are righteous, trusting God to integrate our identity when we consistently relate to the family of God.

Equipping to Work for God

The weakest link in the gathered services of the church surely is in the preparation for re-entry into the world. William Diehl describes one church building he visited where every door leading to the outside had posted above it the words "Servants Entrance."[11] If the Christian is to view life in *diaspora* in unity with life in *ecclesia,* the local church must sustain its members in the ministry of work as much as it now sustains people in the work of the ministry. (William Diehl's *Thank God, It's Monday!* lists some practical suggestions for activities the local church can do to foster support for the ministry of work: weekend retreats, Christian support groups, church programs and so on.)

Three stonemasons were once asked what they were doing. Cutting along a chalk line with mallet and chisel, one said, "I'm cutting this stone." The second said, "I'm earning my pay." The third replied, "Why, I'm building a cathedral."

The products of the three workers *might* have looked the same. Each might have had good or bad reasons for doing an excellent job. What was different was the soul of the worker.

We Christian "stonemasons" must build our cathedral in a society that, along with the form of this world, is both passing away and moving toward its destiny of a new heaven and a new earth. What we need, then, are city saints who can turn a screw on an assembly line for God's glory, and homemakers that will wipe noses or scrub walls and salve hurts for the love of Jesus.

When we have done that, we will not try to put work before ministry or ministry before work, as though one were the cart and the other the horse. All work will be ministry and all ministry, work. And we together will become God's cathedral.

The point of equipping for the *diaspora* is to get Zaphenath-Paneah to say, "I am Joseph" and to get the Josephs to do the work of Zaphenath-Paneah for God. Therefore, one of the most profound equipping questions that one Christian can ask another about both work and mission is this: Where in the world are you?

6. Equipping for Mission: Where in the World Are You?

Mission is simply the this-worldly part of the church's life. Even the biblical image of the church as the body of Christ, if taken seriously, would suggest that the church should imitate what Jesus did with his body: he sacrificed it for a perishing humanity. The church then is expendable. It does not *have* a mission. It *is* mission. It exists by mission as a fire exists by burning.

Some years back, I was impressed by a statement of this theme by Dietrich Bonhoeffer:

I remember a conversation that I had in America 13 years ago with a young French pastor. We were asking ourselves quite simply what we wanted to do with our lives. He said he would like to become a saint (and I think it's quite likely that he did become one). At the time I was very impressed, but I disagreed with him, and said, in effect, that I should like to learn to have faith. For a long time I didn't realize the depth of the contrast. I thought I could acquire faith by trying to live a holy life, or something like it. I discovered later, and I'm still discovering right up to this moment, that it is only by living completely in this world that one learns to have faith. One must completely abandon any attempt to make something of oneself, whether it be a saint, or a converted sinner, or a churchman. . . . By this-worldliness I mean living unreservedly in life's duties, problems, successes and failures, experiences and perplexities. In so doing we throw ourselves completely into the arms of God, taking seriously not our own sufferings, but those of God in the world—watching with Christ in Gethsemane. That, I think, is faith; that is metanoia.[1]

During the persecutions of the second and third centuries, it was the little people, nameless and despised by the cultured observers, who carried the gospel into every possible recess of society. Undoubtedly they did more to prepare for the gospel's conquest of the Greco-Roman world than the bishops, apologists and official missionaries. The pagan critic Celcius says as much in an unintended compliment:

In private houses also we see wool-workers, cobblers, laundry-workers and the most illiterate and bucolic yokels, who would not dare to say anything at all in front of their elders and more intelligent masters. But when they get hold of children in private and some little old women with them, they let out some astounding statements as, for example, that they must not pay any attention to their fathers and school-teachers, but must obey *them;* they say that these talk nonsense and have no understanding, and that in reality they neither know nor are they able to do anything good, but are taken up with mere empty chatter. But *they* alone, they say, know the right way to live and if the children would believe *them,* they would become happy and make their home happy as well.[2]

The church's mission to give itself for the life of the world belongs to the "cobblers" and "yokels" as well as to the theologians and apostles. It is important to understand the unity and diversity of this mission.

The Unity of the Church's Mission
From the Reformation emphasis on two mandates from God—the crea-

tion mandate and the missionary mandate—some dichotomous thinking has arisen. The creation mandate (Gen 1:26-28) calls man (male and female) to be stewards of creation, just as Joseph provided for his family and his neighbors. The creation mandate includes the full range of work experiences from farming to human genetic engineering, from technology to homemaking. God has never revoked this creation mandate (even though sin has made creation itself to groan, Gen 3:17-18; Rom 8:19-23; and human rulers treacherous and unfaithful, Ps 82). Work is therefore good and the Christian is called on to accept God's verdict on creation: "very good."

The unity of the two mandates. Because man failed to keep the first mandate, God gave us in Jesus the missionary mandate, the new creation mandate or, as it is commonly called, the Great Commission (Mt 28:19-20; 1 Pet 2:9; Col 1:28). But what is seldom understood is that God gave us the second mandate in order to restore the first. Evangelism has as its goal the restoration of the whole person in relation to God, to neighbor and to the environment. The goal of mission is to make us fully human, not religious. The gospel announces that without Christ we can never fulfill our calling as keepers of the earth, keepers of the family, keepers of culture and civilization (Heb 2:5-9; Col 1:15-23; Eph 1:21; 3:10). The gospel should enable us to become the best citizens of the world, whether as artists or homemakers or scientists or politicians or educators. Wilbur Sutherland puts the matter succinctly: "To attempt to fulfil the second mandate which, in effect, is evangelism, while at the same time withdrawing from much of life, its pleasures and responsibilities, is to make the gospel of redemption a further occasion to fail with respect to the first mandate."[3]

So the two mandates form a unity. Our call to work to sustain the world and our call to evangelize the world with the message of redemption thorough Christ are both implicit in the life for which Jesus saves us. We are saved in order to fulfill God's original intention.

It is sometimes argued that the Great Commission is a higher priority for the Christian than is the creation mandate. It is said that this priority of the kingdom is evident in the petitions of the Lord's Prayer. The first four speak of God's concerns and the second four about human concerns; all are called to be caretakers of creation, but the Christian is specifically called to advance the kingdom and to serve the King. But, as we have already seen, when we do our work on earth *for God,* the kingdom of God is advanced. Evangelism is the apex of kingdom work, not the whole; the center, not the circumference. The two mandates belong together, for "what God has joined together, let man not separate" (Mt 19:6). If we separate these two mandates, those working like Joseph will be regarded as second-class workers in the kingdom of God. The Bible clearly does not make this distinction.

The unity of mission and vocation. This failure to link our theology of mission with our doctrine of vocation emaciates the theory and practice of the church's mission:

First, Christianity is made private, reduced to personal experience; public and private ethics are divorced. One sad result of this is what (I suspect) has happened in North American culture in the last few dec-

"*Last year we 'reached the world.' This year we're 'sharing and caring.'*"

ades: while more people are overtly evangelical, Christian faith and values seem to have substantially less impact on American culture and public life than before.

Second, mission is disconnected from life. It is normally presented as a cross-cultural effort to reach people elsewhere for Christ. God surely calls people to cross-cultural frontiers, to reach "hidden peoples" and to learn new languages. But the normal mission of Christians is precisely where God has placed us—in our own neighborhood, work world and culture. Indeed, if we have not proved ourselves as missionaries where we live and work, we should not regard ourselves as equipped to go anywhere else. God does not usually call us to do for a stranger what we will not do for a neighbor.

Third, social action and evangelism are separated, the latter elevated above the former. In reality they are both kingdom work and belong together. As Charles Sweazie said, "Social action without evangelism is like sowing grains of sand in the soil; evangelism without social action quickly heads towards superstition."

Christians of the first two centuries shared the gospel of Jesus with their neighbors *and* did what they could to meet the social needs of their society. During the plagues, Dionysius of Alexandria wrote about the ministry of Christians to their neighbors:

> The best of our brethren, some presbyters, deacons, and many of the laity that were exceedingly commended, transferred death to themselves. . . . They took up the bodies of the saints with their open hands and on their bosoms cleaned their eyes and closed their mouths, carried them on their shoulders, and composed their limbs, embraced, clung to them, and prepared them decently, washing and wrapping them up, and ere long they themselves shared in the same offices, those that survived always following those before them. Among the heathen, it was the direct reverse. They repelled those who began to sicken, and avoided their dearest friend.[4]

Fourth, failure to link mission and vocation has also produced an inconsistent definition of worldliness. Religious Christians who restrict vocation to ministry in *ecclesia* often define worldliness as any involvement more than is absolutely necessary in this world's affairs, especially with regard to its social life, its culture and to the "principalities and powers" of its structures. They may raid the world for scalps, but they must not take a place in it.

Not surprisingly, non-Christians consider Christians starved of life and afraid to venture out from the protection of their own religious world. The new creation, as presented by hesitant Christians, seems neither tougher than the old nor more attractive.

What religious Christians fail to realize is that by this very isolation, they become trapped unwittingly in real worldliness. Isolation from society only produces the tragic "religious" worldliness of legalism, asceticism and ritualism. We are freed from the world *in* the world by entering daily into an awareness of God's grace and by walking in the Spirit.

Joseph was a man whose vocation and mission were one. Of him Pharaoh said, "Can we find anyone like this man, one in whom is the spirit of God?" (Gen 41:38).

The Diversity of the Church's Mission
The equipper's task is not merely to help Christians discover the *unity* of ministry and vocation and to live fully in both for the kingdom. The equipper must also help believers to discover and contribute to the diversity of the church's mission by developing each person's unique calling. To the monks at Gethsemane, Thomas Merton said, "Each of us has an irrevocable vocation to be Christ, and the Christ that I am supposed to be is irreplaceable. It has to be my vision of Christ and, if I do not fulfill that, there is going to be something missing forever and forever in the kingdom of Heaven, and each of us knows this and feels this."[5] This statement rings true not only to intuition but to the repeated emphasis of Scripture. Each of us serves the kingdom in a unique and special way: "To each one of us grace has been given as Christ apportioned it" (Eph 4:7).

One secret of equipping Christians for life in dispersion is simply to not disconnect them. The church, like the gathering and dispersion of the blood in the body, is a rhythm. The church gathered must not be separated from the church dispersed any more than the heart and lungs can be separated from the body. Gathered, the blood is cleansed and oxygenated. Sent out, it fights disease and energizes. In the context of a congregation, equipping for mission will therefore have the following four strategic elements.

First, it will discern the body in dispersion. Generally when we "discern" the body, we attempt to find those gifts, ministries and motivations that are significant for our life together. Who is gifted in leading worship? Who has the gift of teaching? Who has the gift of pastoring? Who has the gift of administration? This we ought to do, but without neglecting the other side of ministry.

We need to find where God has sovereignly placed the members of the body when they are *not* together—in what neighborhoods, in what jobs, in what civic responsibilities. These should become a matter of prayer, strategic planning and guided training. Clusters can be formed of people who share a common mission.

Carole, for example, is a nutritionist who is called of God to deal with world food needs and the use and abuse of food in our own society. By God's leading she married a man who teaches advertising and marketing at our local university. Their team effort to expose the dangerous conspiracy of advertising with poor food-consumption habits is their God-appointed mission. It is kingdom work and mission just as is leading a house-group Bible study.

Second, mission will emerge organically. The standard approach to community outreach is to survey the community with the best sociological tools, ascertain the most pressing needs, hire staff to facilitate the program and hope that you get some volunteers. Nothing could be more alien to the New Testament. There the Spirit directed, restrained and empowered. Sometimes Paul was prevented by the Spirit from going to a needy place because God had other plans. Paul had a long-range plan for his mission—to establish a self-propagating Christian church in every major center of the Roman Empire. But the month-by-month implementation was a matter of much spontaneity and Spirit direction. It depended on individuals—like Lydia (Acts 16:13-15)—to take up the mission.

If Jesus is the Head, then surely he can direct his body into mission.

One of the clearest indications of his leadership is his provision of gifts and visions. Recognizing the particular gifts and visions he has given the members of a local church is part of discovering his agenda for mission. Thus, by discerning his body we can anticipate what he wants us to do.

Garth had a vision for day camping as a summer ministry in the community. This was not a project in the minds of the elders, but, as it turned out, it was in the mind of the Lord. Because we know that vision is not limited to the elders, our fellowship has established a development fund in its annual budget to help realize the vision of any member. The concept that mission arises from visions and dreams links mission to individual aptitude and interest and thus encourages the discovery of gifts.

The special mix of spiritual gifts and burdens in each local church is God's way of indicating what their agenda for mission should be. When several members come together in a mission, the whole church may be called to embrace it. Our fellowship has experienced this. We operate two homes. One is Link House, for international students; the other is The Branch, our hostel for traumatized young adults. These two missions arose from heartfelt burdens in the membership rather than from scientific diagnosis of the needs of the city. When it comes to mission, the need is not the call. The call comes from God.

Equipping for mission will also encourage every believer to have around him or her two flocks—one of believers and one of nonbelievers. Each flock would be the significant relationships that God has brought into one's life.

Each flock needs nurture, and the believer must have time to cultivate each set of relationships. Few things inhibit believers' outreach and ministry of work as much as church structures and programs that absorb most of the discretionary time of its members. It would be better to have one gathering Sunday, one house group during the week and to leave the balance of time for believers to relate to their little flocks.

The third element in equipping for mission is the creation of "go" structures. Most of our church structures are "come" structures—they communicate by their existence and style "come and hear," "come and see." They invite people to join the believers, a legitimate expression of the church's mission (see Jn 1:39; 10:40-42; Acts 28:30). As Michael Green has shown, house groups and home meetings are undoubtedly the basic "come" structure to supplement the ubiquitous Sunday service.[6]

There is no question of the value of "come" structures. What is needed is an equal interest in "go" structures, ordered ways for believers to relate in order to reach a particular part of society. The most useful such structure is *the mission house group.* Gordon Cosby has developed this concept fully in his *Handbook for Mission Groups.*[7] The story of one of our own house groups will illustrate the process. It started with people who already had a mission vision. The Cuddefords had a deep interest in foreign missions and in international students. The Jewells had a mission of friendship to those who are mentally ill. The Northeys had a prison ministry. It would have been easier to come together around one mission but the Lord had other plans.

These couples began to support one another and their respective missions in prayer. This was their common ground in Christ. They started to do practical things together. They threw a party for prisoners. They spent a Saturday painting a room at Link House.

They began to spend a lot of time together. The average commitment of this group to be together for prayer, Bible study, fellowship and mission is over six hours each week. They also agreed to spend blocks of time together in retreat.

To further strengthen their commitment to mission, they adopted a covenant to define the shape of their commitment in terms of prayer, service and finances. Out of their own funds they were able to rent an apartment to accommodate prisoners recently released.

It took a long time to form this missions group, now so solid; and they didn't get there without sacrifice and suffering.

Diverse Spiritual Gifting

As well as in the rhythm of gathering and dispersing, the church's diversity in mission is manifest in diverse spiritual gifts. In *The Secular City,* Harvey Cox broke down the church's mission in society along lines established by three Greek words: *diakonia* (which means service), *koinōnia* (which means fellowship) and *kērygma* (which means proclamation or verbal communication).[8] These three words encompass the breadth of charismatic gifting—the ministry of practical service and healing, the ministry of fellowship and the ministry of the Word. The fact that ordination currently only recognizes ministers in the third category shows how restricted our sense of mission is. A closer look at each of these words will help us develop a fuller theology of equipping for mission.

The church's diakonic function is practical service. Dan and Linda were not ordinary immigrants. They faced no language barrier and came to Canada with the promise of a job which would pay over one hundred dollars a week. But the dream vanished when Dan discovered that he was too short for this particular job. Unable to find work, they soon became faceless numbers on the welfare list. They lived with their two small children in a succession of squalid flats and apartments, moving from time to time because they sometimes were unable to pay their rent from the inadequate welfare check. Some of us began to have a ministry with this family in the course of helping them move.

From the other end of the dresser, Dan panted, "The next move is heaven!" This was more than casual banter. Both Dan and Linda had recently tried to commit suicide by turning on their gas oven, only to be interrupted by the visit of a neighbor. Their marriage was punctuated with violent arguments, even fistfights and physical violence, that left in their aftermath self-hatred and remorse. By this time I had shared in their lives sufficiently to know both their simple dignity and their real desperation. Dan may truly have wanted the next move to be heaven, but it wasn't.

This family would be made whole only if the gospel were communicated in terms of their needs and sorrows and hopes. In due course they did come to know Christ—through the church's concern for the whole person.

In the first few centuries A.D. the church was distinguished by its service to society. Some of the areas of social concern were these:

□ *the care of children and infants.* It was said of the Christians, "They do not cast away their offspring."[9]

□ *hospitality.* Deaconries, hospitals and hostelries run by the Christian church were in many cases the only inns for travelers and the only refuge for the weary.

□ *the burial of the dead.* During the Roman Empire, Christians formed the first burial society.

□ *the care of widows and orphans.* Cornelius of Rome "counted besides his 46 presbyters, 7 deacons, 7 sub-deacons, 42 acolytes, 52 exorcists, readers and janitors; not less than 1500 widows!"[10]

□ *the status of women.* The Christian faith has largely brought to pass the movement over the centuries of giving women legal status, the vote and social equality. "Heavens! what women these Christians have!" exclaimed Libanius, hearing the story of the pure and noble life of Anthusa, mother of John Chrysostom.[11]

□ *the establishment of hospitals and universities.* These are children of the church's service.

In the Middle Ages the world was given a new type of social worker in the friar, a new pattern for outdoor ministry in St. Francis and a new model of kingship under St. Louis. Besides being the chief civilizing agency, the church in the Middle Ages "was the chief instrument of social service."[12]

During the revivals of the eighteenth and nineteenth centuries, the evangelists were often the leaders in social· reform. Speaking of John Wesley and his preachers one commentator says: "To a phenomenal degree, these despised itinerant preachers were the heralds of a true Christian democracy; far more than history has yet realized, they did release influences which have affected profoundly the sanest movements for social emancipation throughout the English-speaking world."[13] In the preface to his 1739 hymnbook, Wesley wrote, "The Gospel of Christ knows no religion but social, no holiness, but social holiness."[14]

In short, many of the church's finest deeds throughout history have not simply been individual acts of charity, compassion and good will. Many of them required changing social institutions which served to announce to the principalities and powers the presence of the kingdom (Eph 3:10). We have already seen that part of our kingdom vocation involves dealing with "the powers" at work in society.

Therefore, equipping believers for mission involves supporting some believers in activities that are inescapably complex: working for prison reform, nuclear disarmament, anti-abortion lobbies, appealing for censorship of pornographic literature and movies, working *in* the secular education system for values and standards. All this is being done by evangelicals today, but too often without the full support of their home churches. Equipping must take into consideration the social nature of social action. Halford Luccock has pointed out that "if everyone in town dug a well in his backyard, the result would not be a municipal water system."[15] Saving individuals is not enough.

In *The Social Achievements of the Christian Church*, E. H. Oliver says that the church has a fivefold function as servant: it must exercise its age-long prophetic vocation and serve as conscience to society; it must educate and inspire; it must pioneer new ministries; it must study to seek to prevent rather than to cure; it must transform the helped into helpers.[16]

The church's koinoniac function is fellowship. Tertullian's oft-quoted testimony shows how fellowship itself is part of the church's mission: "It is our care for the helpless, our practice of lovingkindness, that brands us in the eyes of many of our opponents. 'Only look,' they say, 'look how they love one another. . . . Look how they are prepared to die for one another.' "[17]

The church is by nature different from every other society on earth. In Ephesians 2 Paul speaks about the broken wall which formerly divided Jew and Gentile. Out of the two formerly estranged peoples God created one new humanity. Paul implies in this passage that if God can join Jews and Gentiles, then there are no two groups of people that cannot be united in Christ. Markus Barth comments: "When no tensions are confronted and overcome, because insiders or outsiders of a certain class or group meet happily among themselves, then the one new thing, peace, and the one new man created by Christ, are missing; then no faith, no church, no Christ is found or confessed."[18]

It was this koinonia dimension of mission that moved the leaders of Temple Baptist Church in Montreal to seek a credible alternative to the ethnic churches that were springing up. It is well known that churches grow fastest as "you-all" clubs, people speaking with the same twang and having the same background. But our mission is not simply to grow numerically, and fellowship is marked not by the sameness of people but by differences united in Christ. Therefore we formed five ethnic congregations into one Canadian church. We respected the need for ethnic expression, so there were services and ministries in Greek, Italian, Spanish, Armenian and English. At the same time, we called people to join the body of Christ, an international fellowship that witnessed to a new humanity. With banks of earphones on each side of the sanctuary, we simultaneously translated the services on Sunday morning. Once a month we all did our own thing in our own languages. We were never quite sure if it was Babel or Pentecost! But it *was* koinonia.

The church's kerygmatic function is proclamation. But often there is a short in our communication circuit. Most training courses in personal evangelism short out at one of two points. Either they concentrate on mere technique or they train people in an environment foreign to the one in which they live and work. No doubt such training "raids" do something to stimulate faith, boldness and clarity in witness. But I am not convinced that such hothouse training experiences are translated into increased witnessing to neighbors and coworkers. And if it doesn't happen when the Christian really is in the world, is it happening at all?

Once again, the local church is the best training agency in personal evangelism. By its natural rhythm of life, the church moves from worshiping the exalted Lord to serving and living for God in the real world. Small groups are natural networks for praying and encouraging people who are relating to their neighbors.

Evangelistic Bible studies work best with real neighbors. I met a neighbor at a cocktail party and, discovering an interest in eternal things, I later invited him to a group meeting in our home. No one could ever have contrived such a personal and providential rendezvous. Already he had been partly innoculated by the door-to-door religious salesmen and media hucksters.

There is another kind of word ministry to which Christians are called and for which they need to be equipped. It is the prophetic word. Jesus said, "Seek first his kingdom and his righteousness" (Mt 6:33). The church upholds and proclaims the righteousness of God by preaching the gospel of justification by faith which announces God's sentence of forgiveness and grace to wrongdoers. But God's righteousness is also sought by upholding the moral imperatives of the Bible, by insisting on the dignity of the human person, by exposing injustice and by seeking social equality and a more equitable distribution of wealth and resources. This prophetic ministry is not an inferior calling for it fulfills the original creation mandate. The Christian seeks renewal in every area of human dominion: science, art, technology, business, education, medicine, economics and politics.

Common salt is composed of two deadly poisons, sodium and chlorine. Taken separately in sufficient quantity they will destroy life. Together they are essential for life. The church's mission is composed of *both* evangelism and social action and each is deadly without the other. In *this* way we are the salt of the earth.

When we ask whether the salt has lost its savor, we must not inquire only about our spirituality. The salt becomes insipid just as surely when we no longer *do* what Jesus did. Some have specialized in communion and neglected the towel and the basin. Others neglect communion for the towel and basin. Mission requires both.

Decades ago, P. T. Forsyth expressed this enigmatically but thoughtfully: "The largest and deepest reference of the gospel is not to the world and its social problems but to eternity and its social obligation."[19] The church must be equipped to serve in the world precisely because it does not belong to the world. If we start with the world, the church will lose its mission. If we start with God, the church cannot refrain from giving its life for the world. But in such dying we live.

Part IV
Strategy for Equipping the Laity

7. Six Ways to Beat the Solo Ministry Trap

Yertle was a selfish big-headed turtle who decided he was king of the little pond of Salamosond. He decided he couldn't see enough sitting on his throne, so he called some other turtles to stand on each other's backs so that Yertle could sit on his throne at the very top.

The higher he got, the more he wanted to see and consequently the more turtles he had to have beneath him. Thus he kept building his throne by stepping on more and more turtles. At the bottom of this immense pile of turtles was a very little turtle named Mack. Groaning under the terrific load, Mack cried out, "Your majesty, please . . . I don't like to complain. But down here below, we are feeling great pain. I know, up on top, you are seeing great sights. But down here at the bottom we, too, should have rights. We turtles can't stand it."

Yertle bellowed back, "There's nothing higher than me!" But Mack did a very ordinary thing and brought the pile crashing down, Yertle and all. He burped![1]

Is this an unfair picture of the typical solo pastor? Or the superstar pastor? Does the pastor make this pedestal or does someone else? Are a pastor's vistas of spiritual perception gained by aggressively pursuing fulfillment in ministry while being supported by the laity?

I once asked some seminary students from the United States whether they were being taught equipping as the key pastoral model. "That's what we're *taught*," they said, "but the model pastors brought in to the seminary for us to meet are usually superstars."

The pastor as equipper provides a refreshing alternative to the pastor as solo virtuoso. But the full liberation of the laity will require a gracious conspiracy of clergy and laity. As things stand now, it is easier for the pastor to continue to do ministry alone and easier for the laity to rent a shepherd to do it for them. Both need something like a conversion to release them for ministry in the body and through it to the world.

Equipping is not a gift that some people have and others do not. Rather, it is what each of us is called to do with the gift for ministry he or she has. A study of the Greek roots for equipping uncovers six images of the pastor as equipper, six alternatives to Yertle. Rather than treat these images in abstraction from any particular need or ministry of the church, I have chosen to discuss them in connection with one of the most crucial and urgent equipping needs of the modern church: the ministry of women. (Women's ministry is just one aspect where all six need to be applied. Others could have been chosen, but this one well illustrates the principles of equipping.)

The pastor-equipper, and his or her colleagues in church leadership, must seek not so much to equip woman for the work of the ministry, though this must be done. But the real problem is that the church needs to be equipped—prepared, structured, instructed—for women's ministry. Women have access to most of the training resources that men have. What is lacking is opportunity. Speaking for women, Miriam Adeney recently wrote about the need for an extra anointing in relational skills for women wishing to express ministry freely. "It is difficult to maintain smooth balance when we have been bottled up for some time, when our contributions skillfully are ignored, when we lack practice in assertiveness. . . . To relax in negotiations, we women must develop thicker skins and cannier bargaining skills. Meanwhile, let us remember, 'the wisdom that is from above is . . . peaceable, gentle, easy to be entreated' (James 3:17)."[2]

There are actually four Greek words which are used in the New Testament to describe the equipping task: the first is *artios,* a noun which means "complete" or "sound"—used only once in the New Testament in 2 Timothy 3:17. The second is *katartismos,* a noun used once in Ephesians 4:12 where it means preparation. This most closely resembles the dictionary meaning of *equipping*—"making ready or competent for service or action." That is the basic idea of "equipment" or "equipping" or "for the preparation of the saints," as it is variously translated. Third is *katartisis,* a noun which means being made complete. It is used this way in 2 Corinthians 13:9: "Our prayer is for your perfection." Finally, there is *katartizō,* a verb used thirteen times. It means to put in order, to restore and to prepare.[3]

The church needs to be equipped for women's ministry. The following six images of the pastor as equipper provide some insights for doing this. Three of these images are corrective and three are creative. Equipping is first *repairing* something and then *preparing* it for something even better.

The Equipper as Physician
Though *katartismos* ("equipping," "preparing") occurs in the New Testament only once (Eph 4:12), the word has an interesting history as a medical term in classical Greek. [4] A Greek doctor would "equip" a body by putting a bone back into its correct relationship with the other members of the body. By reducing a fracture or realigning a dislocated limb, the doctor "equipped" the patient. The task of an equipping minister is to see that members of Christ's body who are in a broken relationship or are wrongfully connected to the body become correctly related. Paul uses the verb form of the word to exhort the divided Corinthians to "be perfectly united *[katērtismenoi]* in mind and thought" (1 Cor 1:10). It is a pastoral ministry.

Barnabas equips Saul. A biblical example of this equipping function is the ministry of Barnabas to Saul, the converted Pharisee, when he was "out of joint" with the Jewish Christian leaders in Jerusalem. The disciples were afraid of their former persecutor and would not let this strongly gifted new Christian join them. But "Barnabas took him [Saul] and brought him to the apostles. He told them how Saul on his journey had seen the Lord and that the Lord had spoken to him, and how in Damascus he had preached fearlessly in the name of Jesus" (Acts 9:27). Barnabas put the dislocated limb into the socket.

This is precisely what needs to be done in equipping the church for women's ministry. If we deal with women's ministry exclusively as a truth issue or an authority issue or a matter of biblical interpretation or a matter of church order, we may neglect a biblical concern, namely, to get dislocated members back into joint. At the moment, many strong, talented women find it necessary to fulfill their ministry in parachurch organizations and overseas. Years ago, Florence Nightingale, an exceedingly gifted woman, commented on the church's openings for people like herself: "I would have given her my head, my heart, my hands. She would not have them. She did not know what to do with them. She told me to go back and crochet in my mother's drawing room; or if I was tired of that, to marry and look well at the head of my husband's table. . . . She gave me neither work to do for her nor education for it."[5]

Settling this issue is easier if you are not a pastor standing at the door of the church. Looking *out* through the doors, I see a society in social revolution before my very eyes. In Canada a woman was appointed to the highest official post—the office of governor general, the official representative of the Queen. Liberated secular women seeking Christ are often repulsed at finding a church that believes women should be silent, should not teach and should not have authority over men. One such lady said to me, "Your church asks us women to shut our mouths and to open our wombs!" When I tried, in an equipping way, to draw this lady into a full connection with the truth of God in Scripture, I was seen by her as an inflexible conservative.

But standing at the door of the church and looking *in,* I find myself impatient to see women enter into the full inheritance of ministry in the body of Christ. When I hear, as I did recently, of a church in which the elders were petitioned *by the women* not to open the question of women's ministry, I grieve for the body of Christ. To such women I must sound like a liberal. Equipping requires careful, empathetic listening.

I remember the day the Pope declared that it was no longer sinful to eat meat on Fridays. Perplexed, my Catholic neighbor leaned over the back fence and said, "All these years I believed I was doing the right thing in not eating meat!" And perhaps he was. But to be told that something once thought wrong is now right is spiritually confusing. For years many women have remained silent while less gifted men exercised ministry. To tell these women they may now speak and minister and lead, is to threaten spiritual confusion and disillusionment—just as Saul's conversion did. Nothing short of a pastoral ministry will begin the process of equipping the church for the full ministry of women.

The first equipping task in this matter is to do what Barnabas did with Saul. He first had to find out where his brother was, listen to him and believe him. Then he had to take the initiative to relate him to the body so that his gifts could be fully expressed.

Equipping is then a pastoral ministry. It involves working patiently to create relationships where none exist, or to correct awkward or broken ones. The equipper gets the sheep together.

The Equipper as Off-Duty Fisherman

The equipper is also like a fisherman mending his nets in preparation for another night's work. This is the literal use of the verb *katartizō*. James and John "were in a boat with their father Zebedee, preparing *[katartizontas]* their nets" (Mt 4:21). This literal use of the verb *katartizō* has the double meaning of undoing the harm and damage done by previous service and preparing the nets for further service. These nets are not prepared for storage but for another night's work. And they would have been so used if Jesus had not called them to become fishers of men. Equipping a net involves cleaning, mending and folding.[6]

If the nets are not cleaned of seaweed and sticks, the water will not easily pass through. If the nets are not mended of breaks and tears, the fish will pass through. If the nets are not folded, the opportunity to catch fish will pass by because the nets will be too tangled to be of use. The off-duty fisherman's task is as strategic as his on-duty task.

Equipping is putting believers into proper relationship to their service—cleaning, mending and folding their nets. And this preparedness refers to disposition and to heart readiness as much as to training and information.

Titus equips Paul. This second aspect of equipping is illustrated by an episode in Paul's life when he was equipped by one of his younger colleagues. In 2 Corinthians we are given an unusual inner portrait of the great apostle in turmoil: "conflicts on the outside, fears within" (7:5). Having just written a sharp letter of correction to the church at Corinth (1 Cor) Paul was desperate for news of its reception and their response. While waiting for an answer, he was so tangled that he abandoned a fruitful ministry in Asia Minor and went to northern Greece looking for Titus. "But God, who comforts the downcast, comforted us by the coming of Titus" (7:6). Titus comforted Paul's spirit, helped him find strength in God and restored his soul for service again.

One wonders who might have done that for Florence Nightingale, a talented woman whom the church failed to equip. In our fellowship the turning point in this vital ministry of equipping women took place one evening after almost two years of difficult discussion within the eldership. A quotation from the minutes of the previous elders' meeting is the most forlorn entry in our long and fruitful record: "Hours of discussion relapsing into ground covered in the last seventeen months. However, having both extremes aired and all positions between looked at, we are really no further ahead on this issue. At this point nothing new can be unanimously stated to the congregation. More prayer is necessary."

Our nets were ripped, clogged and in a mess. Our eldership operates on unanimity and we seemed to be stuck on this issue. By failing to draw women into full ministry and by failing to say to women content with traditional roles, "Friend, move up to a better place" (Lk 14:10), we found that we were provoking in some women the very anger and ambition we find so alarming. On the other hand we were not willing to conform to a society that proposes interchangeable marriage roles and no sexual differences except the obvious.

The real breakthrough in our elders group came when we realized that we were not trying to change each other's convictions. Rather, we had come to respect each other's integrity within differing scriptural interpretations. What we found after months of laughing, weeping, studying and praying was that we could agree to walk together as elders, even with our differences. As an alternative to agreeing on a principle or policy, we could agree, in love, to share ministry fully with our sisters as we were led by the Holy Spirit. I think that was the night the seaweed was taken out of the net.

The Equipper as Stonemason

This third corrective image comes from the Greek translation of the Old Testament (the Septuagint) which uses the word *katartizō* to translate a Hebrew word used several times in Ezra for the rebuilding of the wall of Jerusalem and the Temple.[7] Judah had been taken into captivity, the walls of Jerusalem had been destroyed and the Temple leveled. The loss of Jerusalem was, they believed, the judgment of God. But under Cyrus the Persian, they were allowed to return to Jerusalem and to rebuild the walls and the Temple. "They are restoring *[katartizō]* the walls and repairing the foundations" (Ezra 4:12). This is but one of several places where *katartizō* is used to describe the work of picking up fallen stones and putting them back into an ordered state.

Thus equipping is putting believers into their correct order. It is harmonizing them with what they once were, what they were created by God to be and to what in God's sight they now are. In Galatians 6:1 *katartizō* is used for the equipping of one trapped in sin: "You who are spiritual should restore *[katartizete]* him gently."

As our fellowship went about the task of studying the entire Bible on the matter of women's ministry, we discovered that the highly controversial passage in 1 Timothy 2, in which Paul says that women are not to teach and not to have authority over men, is really a passage about church order. The Ephesian church was in shambles, like the wall in Jerusalem. From 2 Timothy it appears that false teaching was rampant and the women were the last to abandon this false doctrine. They were pushing not just to teach publicly themselves but to teach what would lead people astray, just as Eve had done so long ago (1 Tim 2:14). In the interest of restoring order in the community, Paul tells Timothy how to equip this particular church in this extreme situation. The situation is unique but there are timeless truths to be mined from the passage.

When they pray, the men are to "lift up holy hands in prayer, *without anger or disputing*" (2:8). Then he turns to the women and exhorts them "to dress modestly" (2:9), to learn with a "peaceable spirit" and in "full submission" (2:11, submission not to the men but to correct teaching), "to refrain from teaching" (2:12, the best reading of the text would prohibit these women from teaching even other women), and not to express a domineering authority over men (for the special word for "authority," used only here, has the meaning of domineering[8]). The men were not to have domineering authority over the women either.

This was a devastated church. The men and women needed to be reconciled, eased back into proper relationship with each other. As we struggled with this passage, I was thankful that we did not have men disputing and praying with anger. Nor did we have women who were teaching false doctrine and attempting to domineer men. Our problem arose from the fact that there were gifted women who were not exercising their gifts on behalf of the whole fellowship. Our concern to preserve sexual differences even in church structure and leadership had resulted in an unscriptural imbalance. While it was the common conviction of our church that only men should serve as elders, we had not found other structural ways of giving women full opportunity to express their gifts in teaching, leading worship and other nonelder functions.

Generally, the wives of the elders were satisfied with the arrangement. But as more than one single woman in our fellowship observed, the wife of an elder has no difficulty finding her place in the body. She has a direct line to the center of influence, humanly speaking. One single woman expressed it more diplomatically when she asked, with some sensitivity, "How can the women's decision-making responsibility be given more legitimacy when all the elders are affected by the opinions of their wives?" At Marineview we were not yet liberated enough, in a good scriptural sense, to need the kind of equipping that Paul sought to give to the church at Ephesus. We needed further equipping in order that our members—particularly the women—could be free to minister to the body as God intended.

But equipping is not only corrective, it is creative, as the next three images propose. The first three were repairing images, the next three are preparing images.

The Equipper as Potter

Another meaning of *katartizō* is to create or to form.[9] It suggests the image of a potter fashioning clay. In Romans 9:22, Paul speaks of objects prepared *(katērtismena)* for destruction and compares these with objects prepared for glory. In the letter to the Hebrews we read, "A body you prepared *[katertisō]* for me" (Heb 10:5). After believers have experienced some suffering, God "will himself restore you *[katartisei]* and make you strong, firm and steadfast" (1 Pet 5:10). The God of peace will "equip you with everything good for doing his will" (Heb 13:21).

Equipping is building into people what they need to function effectively as servants of God in the church and in the world. This is God's work in which we have a share. And such molding by God takes place primarily when people are steeped in the Word of God "so that the man of God may be thoroughly equipped for every good work" (2 Tim 3:17). People cannot be formed by the Word of God unless they appropriate the Word for themselves. To this end, some churches have found it useful to devise an integrated plan for Bible learning. According to this plan, the same passage is studied individually, in small groups and in the Sunday sermon. This is an equipping plan that aims at biblical obedience rather than Bible knowledge. At Marineview, we write our own study guides, which has turned out to be a good equipping tool.[10]

A splendid biblical illustration of the potter principle is Aquila and Priscilla's equipping of Apollos. Apollos was intelligent, fervent and teachable, but he knew only the baptism of John (Acts 18:25). Seeing this, Aquila and Priscilla had the good sense to meet with this young preacher in a private setting so as not to threaten him. They "explained to him the way of God more accurately" (18:26). So effective was this situational Bible learning that when Apollos was sent off on a mission "he was a great help to those who by grace had believed" (18:27).

As the elders at Marineview sought to mold our fellowship according to scriptural teaching concerning women's ministry, we were confronted with a very challenging task. The big problem is not with what the Bible says about women's ministry but what we *think* it says. We developed a process of discovery learning: First, as elders we committed ourselves to thorough Bible study over many months. We studied every text from Genesis to Revelation that related to the issue because we did not consider the matter settled by the statement "there is neither . . . male nor female, for you are all one in Christ Jesus" (Gal 3:28), or by "I do not permit a woman to teach" (1 Tim 2:12). We read widely on the subject and produced our own position papers. It was more important that we make our own discoveries than to accept someone else's.

In this process of discovery we next invited the entire congregation to join with the elders in searching the Scriptures. (Unfortunately, the elders' failure to reach unity delayed this second step too long.) We reproduced various papers on different sides of the issue and held a "priesthood of men and women" day. The entire day was spent exploring what Scripture says and the history of the issue. Godly leaders were brought in to represent more extreme positions than our elders themselves held.[11] We anticipated that young Christians would find it disheartening and confusing to see respected Christian leaders disagreeing on an important issue. But we believed the diversity needed to be confessed. We bathed the day in prayer.

Third, we invited the entire congregation to join in an integrated curriculum study of 1 and 2 Timothy. We knew that the greatest difficulty would arise over 1 Timothy 2 and the women's issue. All this we did before we had an "elders' policy." The Bible belongs to the people not to the leadership, and we hoped that fresh light would break from the Word through the study of passages by the entire fellowship.

The elders adopted no policy. We were not closed to women teaching the entire congregation—this was the big issue at Marineview. We were prepared to ask any appropriate woman to address the body. But we were not prepared to make a special policy about it. We would deal with each Sunday and each person on an individual basis, rather than state a fixed policy.

But that was not the end of the matter. Nor was it the only way in which we were called to equip the church for women's ministry. We were not only potters shaping people in the Word but people responsible for the public modeling of Christian life and ministry.

The Equipper as Parent

As a father of three I know too well how parents unintentionally become models for their children. A psychiatrist friend tells me that children imitate what they see us enjoy. But my children imitate a lot of other things as well. My most ridiculous habit is to walk around the house brushing my teeth—no matter who is there! It is a trait that will undoubtedly be passed on to the third and fourth generations.

Jesus spoke of the disciple-master relationship as essentially one of imitation. It is not so much that trained disciples *know* what the master does. Rather, when they are "fully trained *[katērtismenos]*" they will be *like* their teacher (Lk 6:40). Jesus did not train the Twelve in school; he lived with them. *Equipping is an imitation process in which we fashion people into the image of Christ.* To do this, people need many models, preferably in the context of the local church. Each of us is only a fraction of the image of Christ. We do not want people to conform to a fraction.

I learned this from the postgraduate student from India I mentioned earlier. For the first few months of Pravin's Christian life I spent half a day each week with him reading the Bible and praying. Then I noticed that he was becoming like me, too much like me. He was absorbing my intellectualism and was losing his boldness. Why did he not copy my good points exclusively? Quickly, I got him into the full body of Christ. I delight in that today he is a model for me. Even a superlative pastor could only be a fraction of Christ's image. Every believer willing to share his or her life and to be vulnerable can participate either consciously or unconsciously in equipping others.

Equipping the church for women's ministry requires modeling by mature women. Many women at Marineview told us that there were few models of women in public ministry. Denying women the privilege of public teaching in the fellowship was a negative symbol. But we could not find a positive one to express the five timeless truths we had derived from a careful study of the Scriptures. On these five truths the elders had come to full agreement: First, charismatic gifting for ministry is given by the Spirit to men and women without discrimination. Second, differences between men and women—as difficult as it is to define these absolutely—were nevertheless intrinsic to creation itself and were to be respected in the life of the church; men were to minister as men, and women as women. Third, our reading of the epistles and passages relating to church order suggested that *some* continuation of the Old Testament pattern of male headship in marriage and synagogue was desirable in the church (though we would not say how each church should work this out). Fourth, church leadership should model commendable patterns of husband-wife relationships within marriage. Fifth, these truths and concerns need to be symbolized in the life of the church without slavishly conforming to tradition or maintaining an empty symbol.

In Paul's day head coverings, for example, were a statement of marital relationship, of honoring the husband. When first-century women came to church with their heads uncovered, it was as scandalous as it would be to take off wedding rings in church today, or for women to wear only men's clothing, arguing that there is no longer male or female in Christ. Wearing veils or head coverings today has no significance. Therefore we would not make an absolute of this passing social custom. That would be to take the Scripture literally but not seriously.

More to the point, we had discovered that the word *exousia* ("authority"), which Paul uses in 1 Corinthians 11:10, is more likely the authority of the woman who is rightly related to her husband to pray and prophesy, than the husband's authority over her.[12] "For this reason, and because of the angels, the woman ought to have a sign of authority [*exousia*] on her head." We could not expect the Scriptures, which arise from diverse historical and cultural settings, to come to a common cultural meeting point for us. So we were left with the creative task of finding a way to model what we believed. And we had nothing left to do it with than ourselves. We had to model in our husband-wife relationships, brother-sister relationships in the family of God, the unity and the difference, the nurturing, serving headship and the responsive respect. As people entered our community, they would have opportunity to judge that a given woman was qualified to minister in some public way because of her relationship with her husband, or to the men in the fellowship. Likewise, the male teachers qualified themselves for public ministry by conforming to the New Testament image of the loving, serving husband-leader. Once more we were discovering that equipping has more to do with character development than information gathering.

The Equipper as Project Person

Downstairs my daughter is poring over the last few pieces of a fascinating German jigsaw puzzle. It is a huge and complicated picture of the city of Nuremberg with walls, ramparts, towers and dozens of seemingly identical brick homes. Inevitably there is a blue, cloudless sky. The cry, "I got it!" is my final clue to biblical equipping. For three days the puzzle has been incomplete. Now it is, so to speak, equipped. The equipper, like my daughter, is a project person.

"Our prayer is for your perfection *[katartisin],*" Paul says (2 Cor 13:9, the only place in the New Testament where this particular noun form is used). Clearly, this does not mean sinless perfection. Rather it means completion.[13] Two verses later Paul uses the verb form, "that all may be put right *[katartizesthe]* with you" (2 Cor 13:11 NEB). The same idea of fitting in the missing pieces to accomplish wholeness and completion is implied by the context of Ephesians 4:12: the equipment of the saints is toward growth, toward completion *(teleios),* toward stature in Christ, toward fullness in Christ.

Equipping is putting believers into right relationship with the goal of the faith and seeking their completion by supplying missing dimensions. It is a highly creative and personalized ministry that does not lend itself to a program or a standardized approach.

The great mystery of the gospel for Paul was that Jews and Gentiles *together* were "heirs" and "members of one body." He wanted to equip them toward that goal. He equipped the Gentile church by introducing them to the riches of their Jewish inheritance in Christ: the law, the promises, the covenants, the patriarchs and the human ancestry of Christ (Rom 9:5). He equipped the Jewish church by collecting money from the Gentile believers to give to the poor Jewish saints in Jerusalem. Presenting this gift in Jerusalem at the feast of Pentecost was tantamount to equipping the church toward its goal: complete equality and mutuality in Christ. Therefore he expected to leave Jerusalem for Rome "in the full measure of the blessing of Christ" (Rom 15:29). Each was, in a sense, the missing piece to the other's puzzle. Only together could they be complete.

When we tried to equip Marineview Chapel for women's ministry, we discovered that in certain respects we did not know where we were going or by what fixed points to orient ourselves. With respect to just about everything, including women's ministry, we were somewhere between Eden and the New Jerusalem. We had not reached the church's goal—complete unity and maturity in Christ. Equipping is an orienting ministry. The equipper makes sure the sheep know where they are going.

Paul based his view of male leadership on the creation story. He found in the fact that Eve succumbed to temptation before Adam some special significance, at least for Ephesus (1 Tim 2:13-14). But elsewhere he says that *in the Lord* it is different: "In the Lord, however, woman is not independent of man, *nor is man independent of woman.* For as woman came from man, so also man is born of woman. But everything comes from God" (1 Cor 11:11-12). We at Marineview are a people in pilgrimage; every local church is, and so is the whole church in history. We live in a fallen world. We ourselves will not be completely saved until we reach the New Jerusalem. Therefore, Adam's rule over Eve (Gen 3:16) will not be eliminated by a secular liberation movement or by a church symposium on sexuality. Male rule and female resistance to that rule are deeply ingrained.

But do we want to orient the *goal* of our church life on a curse? Sin has marred the perfect unity and complementarity of male and female in Eden before sin entered the family (Gen 2:18, 23-25). But we should aim at the goal not the failure. There is no way back to that perfect unity of Adam and Eve before the Fall. We must go all the way through history toward complete unity in Christ. We are not there yet but we should make sure we are on the way. The tension of living where we are in the story of salvation is not eliminated by insisting that men must rule over women. Nor can it be resolved by pretending that in this life we are free from the need for structures of leadership and responsiveness that reflect creational differences.

That a gracious equality can exist *at this point in our development* within differing spheres of responsibility and authority is suggested by a contemporary example. At her marriage the Queen of England promised to obey her husband; but at her coronation, he swore allegiance to her.[14] Rather than looking backward in our church order by modeling ourselves after Adam and Eve while they were being expelled from the garden, we should look forward to the complete harmony of the sexes that will exist in the New Jerusalem. This will be nothing less than the gracious complementarity and unity that existed in Eden (Gen 2:18, 23-25). I once heard an old saint say that we gained more on Calvary than we lost in Eden. I wonder now if he really believed that we gain more unity between the sexes through Calvary than we lost in Eden. Equipping insists that we move forward, not backward. Or if our look is backward, it must be to the original plan of God before sin marred it. We are equipping the church to attain complete unity in Christ (Eph 4:13). We are not there yet. But the equipper wants to be there.

This matter of disarming the battle of the sexes and putting the pieces together in the right way and at the right time is really a jigsaw puzzle. I am reminded of a line in John Le Carré's novel *Smiley's People:* "Don't force the pieces, he warned himself. Store them away. Patience. But how to be patient when he had so little time."[15] Some do not want to finish the puzzle; they like it better in pieces, incomplete. Others are so impatient that they force the pieces. The equipper, working with a growth model, humbly shares with the Lord the task of putting the pieces together to complete the picture the right way at the right time.

This last image of the equipper completes the six alternatives: physician (the pastoral ministry), fisherman (the personal ministry), stonemason (the structural ministry), potter (the instructional ministry), parents (the modeling ministry) and project person (the orienting ministry).

The problem with the modern church is not so much the ministry as it is the one-ministry man. Leaders tend to think there is only one way they can exercise their gifts or express their leadership. These six scriptural images broaden the concept of leadership. There is no super-equipper who can do all six. But together—pastor and people—we can!

The ultimate alternative to the solo minister as head of the church, Yertle on top of Mack the layperson, is Christ the Head, underneath serving and over all ruling. A published interview between Gene Getz and Larry Richards brings the matter home. I wish to identify myself, in reporting this, with the thoroughgoing supernaturalism that Larry Richards expresses in his belief that Jesus is the true Leader of the church—though neither he nor I would wish to eliminate human leadership in the role of underequipper.

Getz begins by saying, "I have a story I think illustrates beautifully the need for more careful management as the church grows. Alvin Toffler, in his latest book, *Third Wave,* speaks of the modern symphony orchestra being born in the passage from an aristocratic to a democratic culture in the eighteenth century. The small salons were replaced by larger and larger halls, which demanded greater volume—thus, more instruments and more players. At first the orchestra was leaderless, or the leadership was casually passed around among the players. Later, the players were divided into departments, instrumental sections, each contributing to the overall output of the music, each coordinated from above by a manager, the conductor.

"The orchestra calls for a great sense of concern for aesthetics, unity, harmony, beauty, and oneness; and in many respects reflects what should happen in the body of Christ: it, too, should produce a beautiful symphony. It also illustrates that when a church is relatively small, it can be somewhat leaderless. But as the church grows, it must be divided into certain kinds of departments. There needs to be overall coordination through good management. But we *must not* lose the concept of total participation, of multiple leadership, of body function, or organism!"

Richards responds by saying, "It's a beautiful illustration. I only have one comment: We probably will disagree on who is the conductor."[16]

8. The Case for the Voluntary Clergy

I leaned over the restaurant table to make a request of my friend Gene Thomas, businessman-Bible teacher-tentmaker from Boulder, Colorado. "Gene, would you spend some time with one of my students at Regent College? He's trying to make up his mind whether to go into the professional pastoral ministry or to return to business as a tentmaking minister."

"Tell him to join a monastic order!" Gene said with a wry smile. "Who would want to be a tentmaker?"

Indeed, who would? I define tentmaking as giving oneself *primarily* to ministry while supporting oneself by other work. In 1930 Roland Allen wrote about this biblical option under the awkward title *The Case for the Voluntary Clergy.*[1] If the title is awkward, so is the reality.

Because only part of Allen's works are available in print, I have constructed an imaginary interview with him. Through his books, he is available to help us think through a leadership transformation in the contemporary church.[2]

Roland Allen's early ministry years follow a fairly normal pattern for an Anglican clergyman. At twenty-seven (1895) he went to China as a missionary of the High Church Society for the Propagation of the Gospel. He returned home as an invalid in 1903 and became vicar of Chalfort St. Peter in Buckinghamshire, a post he resigned in 1907. Thereafter he held no official Anglican office. He spent his remaining years living as closely as possible to the ideal of a voluntary clergyman. In 1932 he retired to Kenya where he died in 1947.

To feel the revolutionary force of Allen's thesis we need to understand the arguments against tentmaking today. I heard many of them when I supported myself in carpentry. They are very persuasive.

It is said, for example, that the idea of paid leadership means that a gifted and trained individual is entirely available to the work of the ministry undistracted by other work.

It is also said that leadership in the church today requires leaders who are thoroughly trained in Scripture, theology, philosophy, ethics and ministry methodology. It is impractical and too expensive for the church to give this training to the so-called laity. A corollary charge is that the lack of theological education in tentmaking ministries will breed heresy and false teaching. The seminary is the guardian of truth.

Further, salary and support imply accountability and control. Tentmakers will be less committed and more independent since their livelihood would never be threatened by a falling out with their coworkers in the church. Also, the pressures of modern life and the increasing demand made on professionals or business persons require someone available to minister by proxy.

Professional expectations in all other professions must be matched by expertise, credentials and sophistication in the public leadership of the church. Who would go to a rank amateur for marriage counseling? Most people will not listen to a lay preacher or respect his counsel. They are not interested in amateurism.

Others say that tentmaking is an option for a celibate person like Paul but not for a married person trying to raise a family. The family vocation is too demanding for tentmakers.

Churches that are growing fastest and are most successful have strong professional leadership and staff specialists to meet various ministry needs. Professional leadership works.

Finally I heard that tentmaking was fine as an option for the early church but we are not bound to copy the apostle's obedience or to limit the church of the first century. What works best for us is surely what the Lord of the church wants today. The tentmaking of Paul and Aquila and Priscilla is not normative for us today.

An Interview with Roland Allen

Paul: Having been a missionary in China from 1895 until 1903 and then for a few years in an English parish, you bring to the matter of church leadership a rich background of experiences. However, do you think there is some truth in the charge made to you that times have changed and your methods and principles are out of date?

Roland: I can only repeat "This is the way of Christ and his apostles."[3]

Paul: But in claiming a view of mission work and ministry that is patterned after Christ and the apostles, especially Paul, you must admit that people wandered around the world doing the most slipshod ministry in the name of the apostle himself.

Roland: What has happened is that people have adopted fragments of St. Paul's method and have tried to incorporate them into alien systems. Either we must drag down St. Paul from his pedestal as the great missionary, or else we must acknowledge that there is in his work that quality of universality.[4]

Paul: But it seems to me that in proposing a voluntary clergy you are doing that very thing: incorporating a Pauline model into an alien system. You are a priest in the Church of England and a high churchman at that!

Roland: I admit that I am calling for a reformation of the present system. That reformation is the ordination after the ancient and biblical order of people who maintain themselves by their own trade and profession, whatever it may be.[5]

Paul: Your church tradition, like most church traditions, forbids the ordination of people engaged in earning their own livelihood by what we call secular occupations. What's wrong with that practice?

Roland: It makes void the word of Christ and is opposed to his mind when he instituted the sacraments for his people.[6]

Paul: While you claim that your practice is biblical, apostolic and catholic,[7] I wonder if you are not more moved by the practical impossibility of getting enough ordained priests to the mission field to administer the sacraments.

Roland: We will never establish the church and fulfill the worldwide mission by sending out professional clerics and money from England. But if we could accept apostolic guidance, we could meet the whole need everywhere at home and abroad.[8]

Paul: So you are not simply proposing that several "part-timers" can, if necessary, replace one "full-timer"?

Roland: The distinction between the stipendiary [remunerated] and

"It happens whenever the pastor asks for volunteers."

voluntary clergy is not a distinction between men who give their whole time to the service of God and his church and men who give part of their time to that service, but a distinction between one form of service and another. Both stipendiary and voluntary clergy ought to be serving God and the church all the time in all that they do; but the service which the church needs that each should do for God and for her is not the same. The hedge round the clergy is a very high and well-cultivated one . . . and consequently the restriction of ordination generally to men trained from youth within that hedge inevitably results in the clergy being more or less out of touch with the common experiences of common men. The voluntary cleric, on the other hand, carries the priesthood into the marketplace and the office.[9]

Voluntary Leadership

Paul: You use the word "voluntary" for what I call tentmakers. But is not the remunerated minister in spirit a volunteer?

Roland: We commonly speak of "voluntary workers," meaning people who not only offer their services of their own free will, but also offer their services free of all charge, gratis, as opposed to people who are paid, or receive stipends or allowances, for the work done by them. The term implies nothing derogatory of the service of men who for quite good and sufficient reasons receive stipends.[10]

Paul: So then professionalism, depending on workers with stipends, is for you *both* untrue and strategically unwise?

Roland: Our system is opposed to the conception of the church which the apostles received from Christ, and to the practice by which St. Paul, of whose work God has given us the fullest account, established the churches.[11]

Paul: How did the church come to depend on our clergy system?

Roland: The stipendiary system grew up in settled churches and is suitable for some settled churches only at some periods. But for expansion, for the establishment of new churches, it is the greatest possible hindrance.[12]

Paul: What do you mean by "hindrance"?

Roland: It is a hindrance because it makes the expansion of the church dependent on sufficient financial resources. What is quite clear is that in the apostolic age the establishment of the church with its proper ministers did not depend at all on the provision of a stipend which might set the ministers free from the common toil. The apostles and their successors did ordain men regardless of stipends.[13]

Paul: But would it not be better to permit a gifted and trained individual to give himself undistractedly to the work of the ministry? If a person does something well, should he not do it all the time?

Roland: Not necessarily. Our conception of vocation is one-sided and narrow. We have made a vocation to service into a vocation to a profession.[14] The apostolic conception of the clergy, their work and their relation to the church, is utterly different from ours.[15]

Whom Do We Ordain?

Paul: Surely you are not saying that the apostles wanted the church to be leaderless.

Roland: The question here is not a question of the necessity or the desirability of an ordered ministry. It is agreed that the church ought to be organized with clergy properly ordained. It is not the maintenance of an ordered ministry which conflicts with Christ's commands, but the tradition which restricts ordination.[16]

Paul: Restricts it to what? To the called, the trained and the equipped?

Roland: We have ceased to ordain the type of person described in the Holy Bible. We have ceased to believe that God calls such people to serve in the sacred ministry of his church.[17]

Paul: You must be referring to Paul's instructions in 1 Timothy 3:2-7 and Titus 1:6-9 where the apostle describes the qualities of the bishop, overseer or elder.

Roland: Yes, but we do not dream of using these as standards for ordination. We delight in drawing pictures of the ideal priest, the ideal missionary, the ideal teacher, the ideal pastor. The apostle is not doing that. He is setting up a very practical rule for his followers. He does not say: This is the ideal which you must set before your young clergy; he says: This is the kind of man you must look for and ordain.[18]

Paul: How is that different from what is commonly done?

Roland: Take first the apostle's demand that the candidate be of mature age and proven experience: we commonly ordain the young and inexperienced.[19]

Paul: Are you saying that the qualities needed for church leadership cannot be gotten at seminary?

Roland: If we analyze the passages you just cited, we are struck at once by the great emphasis on moral qualities. Five are personal virtues: temperate, sober-minded, orderly, gentle, not a lover of money. Six are social virtues: first, at home; constant to one wife, ruling the children well, given to hospitality; second, abroad as well as at home; no brawler, no striker, not contentious. Two refer to reputation: first, generally, without reproach; and second, particularly, in the eyes of non-Christians. One is a moral-intellectual power: apt to teach. One is experience: not a novice.[20]

Paul: Are we ordaining the wrong people?

Roland: I went one day into a synod office in Canada. I found there two men: the one was a young theological student, the other a man of about fifty years of age who told me that for fifteen years, when he was farming on the prairie, he held services in his own house for his neighbors. They had a celebration of the Holy Communion two or three times a year when a priest passed that way.

I looked at those two men and I could not help asking myself why the bishop was going to ordain the one and why he has not ordained the other. If spiritual experience is desirable for a priest, which of these two men had the largest spiritual experience? Which of those two men most commanded respect? Which of them had the best and strongest social influence?[21]

Paul: But in our kind of world it is important for a church to be trained theologically, philosophically and methodologically. Since it costs, on the average, about six thousand dollars a year to train a theological student, it is impractical and too expensive to give this training to the laity.

Roland: There is a difference between the holding fast of the faith of a man tried in the furnace of life, and the soundness in the faith of a youth fresh from a theological school. The apostle said nothing whatever about readiness to pass an intellectual test in which the power of a verbal memory is prominent, and readiness to resign all other means of living.[22]

Workers and Their Wages

Paul: Roland, you emphasize the importance of *not* earning your living by the gospel. Didn't Christ himself send out the seventy with the words: "the worker deserves his wages" (Lk 10:7)?

Roland: Those passages do not refer to the settled presbyters or bishops of whom the apostle is writing to Timothy and Titus.[23]

Paul: Surely you are not saying that *no one* must be supported in ministry?

Roland: The church unquestionably needs some men who give themselves wholly to prayer and the ministration of the Word and sacraments, and such men must be supported by the faithful. She needs also some men whose time is wholly occupied with the care of parishes, and these she must maintain. She needs also scholars who give their whole time to study, and these she must maintain. [24]

Paul: Then what is the problem?

Roland: There are countless small groups of Christians needing pastors, which cannot afford to maintain clergy or provide them with sufficient occupation to save them from the temptations of idleness.[25]

Paul: And I suppose this is even more true overseas on the mission field.

Roland: It would be better to teach a few men to call upon the Lord for themselves than to fill a church with people who have given up idolatry, slavishly and unintelligently, and have acquired a habit of thinking that it is the duty of converts to sit and be taught and to hear prayers read for them in the church by a paid mission agent.[26]

Paul: You are not saying, then, that what we call tentmaking must replace what the church calls clergy?

Roland: All sensible men would know that the church needs both. [27]

Paul: But the *ordination,* the public recognition, of voluntary clergy, would tend to destroy the importance of trained, separated and supported ministers.

Roland: The ordination of voluntary clergy, so far from bringing the service of stipendiary clergy into disrepute, would exalt it; because the stipend would drop into its proper place as a mere accident, and vocation to serve would stand out clearly in its purity.[28]

Paul: But Paul told Timothy that "the elders who direct the affairs of the church well are worthy of double honor, especially those whose work is preaching and teaching" (1 Tim 5:17). Since the Greek word for honor means a physician's honorarium for services, we have an apostolic command that teaching elders should be supported.

Roland: We have made of Christ's ordinance and the apostolic exhortation to the faithful a divine command that those who serve the altar *must* live of the altar, and those who preach the gospel *must* live of the gospel (unless they have private means); which is absurd. [29]

Paul: Didn't Paul lay down the law for the clergy in 1 Corinthians 9:14 that "those who preach the gospel should receive their living from the gospel"?

Roland: It is unquestionable that St. Paul himself earned his own living at certain times by the labor of his hands, and that he quoted the ordinance of the Lord, to which you have referred, not as a law inviolable and immutable, but as a permission which he himself declined to use.[30]

Paul: Didn't that all substantially change in the centuries following the apostolic age? And for good reasons?

Roland: For the practice of the church in the centuries following the apostolic age, we may notice first a sentence in the second book of the Apostolic Constitutions, which, whatever the date of composition, now represents a very early tradition. The apostles are urging the duty of diligent work upon young people of the church and they appeal to their example. "We ourselves, besides our attention to the word of the Gospel, do not neglect our inferior employments. For some of us are fishermen, some tentmakers, some husbandmen, that so we may never be idle."[31]

Paul: Was that an isolated case in the second and third centuries or was tentmaking the norm?

Roland: Socrates the historian writes: "With respect to Spyridon, so great was his sanctity while a shepherd that he was thought worthy of being made a Pastor of men; and having been assigned the bishopric of one of the cities of Cyprus named Trimithus, on account of his extreme humility, he continued to feed his sheep during his incumbency of the bishopric . . . such characters adorned the Churches in the time of the Emperor Constantine."

But that the clergy in humbler positions regularly earned their living by handicrafts is proved by a letter written by Basil the Great, Bishop of Caesarea in Cappadocia, a letter generally assigned to the year A.D. 375. In it he says: "Although our clergy do seem very numerous, they are men inexperienced in traveling because they never traffic and prefer to live not far away from home, the majority of them plying sedentary crafts whereby they get their daily bread."

There is also an interesting inscription on a tomb in Ancyra: "Here sleeps the servant of God, Theodorus, presbyter of the saints and silversmith, the friend of all," which suggests the same thing.[32]

Paul: It is easier for us to imagine tentmaking elders, what you call voluntary clergy, giving leadership in small churches or in missionary situations. Larger churches must have required what we call full-time ministers.

Roland: Take for example the way in which Sozomen speaks of Zeno, who was Bishop of Majuma (that is, Gaza) at the end of the fourth century. Sozomen says that Zeno, "by pursuing his trade of weaving linen, continued to earn the means of supplying his own wants and of providing for others. He never deviated from this conduct till the close of his life, although he exceeded all other priests of that province in age, and although he presided over the people and property of *the largest Church*."[33]

Paul: Surely it is not so one-sided a matter in the ancient documents of the church? What are the exceptions?

Roland: In the Apostolic Canons there appears a direction which at the first glance seems to conflict with this. "Let not a bishop, presbyter or deacon take upon himself worldly cares, otherwise let him be deposed."[34]

Paul: Isn't that an argument for the separated, supported ministry?

Roland: No. This addresses itself to two abuses to which the clergy were specially tempted: (1) they were tempted to neglect their spiritual duties in order to wander out of their provinces in search of gain; (2) they were tempted to make money by managing other people's property. In A.D. 393, in the Council held at Hippo, it is directed: "Let no bishop, presbyters and deacons be agents or managers of private estates, nor seek their livelihood by any such business as shall make it necessary for them to wander abroad or to be absent from their ecclesiastical duties."[35]

Paul: So it was not the mere fact of secular employment, but secularity of motive and tone that is condemned.[36] If the remunerated leader is in danger of being a hireling, the tentmaking leader is in danger of being a worldling.

Roland: Sulpicius Severus, who wrote in Gaul at the end of the fourth century in his *Historia Sacra,* draws a lurid picture of their greed: "They cultivate estates, they brood over gold, they buy, they sell; in everything they are wholly given to gain."[37]

Paul: The issue then is the inwardness of the tentmaker, his generosity of spirit, and his freedom from the love of money, not his freedom from gainful employment. Tentmaking was assumed to be the norm.

Roland: That these decrees were not intended to prevent the clergy from earning their living by honest toil is proved by the decrees of the Fourth Council of Carthage, which definitely direct them to do so. The 51st canon reads: "Let a cleric however learned in the word of God get his livelihood by a craft"; the 52nd, "Let a cleric procure his food and raiment by a craft, or by agriculture without interfering with his official duty"; the 53rd, "Let all clerics who are strong enough to work learn both crafts and letters." These canons became the rule for the church over wide areas, and for a long period of time, and the 53rd is quoted as authoritative in England in the eighth century by Ecgbert, archbishop of York.[38]

Vocation and Pay

Paul: You make a lot of the danger of greedy tentmakers in the early church. Isn't the problem today that the supported ministry is not well enough paid to attract workers into the work?

Roland: That is the dilemma on the horns of which a stipendiary system impales us. It is impossible to find a stipend which suffices for the good and discourages the weak. [39]

Paul: You mean by "weak," I suppose, those who would seek the profession because of money. Many think it is not that attractive.

Roland: Worldly-minded people look upon it as a "rotten" profession because it is badly paid. It is possible to argue that the poverty of the profession saves it from degenerating into a mere profession. [40]

Paul: If one is not likely to be corrupted by a large income, why would a clergyman choose, in your phrase, to be voluntary?

Roland: There are, indeed, many people who feel that to make their vocation to the sacred ministry a means of earning money is for them a sort of simony. Such people the church instantly and unhesitatingly rejects.[41]

Paul: Why?

Roland: We seek recruits for a profession; the apostles were selecting leaders for a definite local church.[42]

Paul: What difference does it make?

Roland: St. Paul ordained as elders members of the church to which they belonged. He did not establish a provincial school to which all candidates for ordination must go, and from which they might be sent to minister to congregations in any part of the province. The elders were really of the church to which they ministered. They were at home. They were known to the members of their flock. If they received any pecuniary support, they received it from people who supported them because they felt the need of their undivided and uninterrupted care. Thus the bond between the elders and the church to which they ministered was extremely close.[43]

Paul: What is wrong with sending in a minister to fill a pastoral vacancy?

Roland: When a good cleric is sent to a new parish he begins by trying to make friends with the people. But is it not strange that a society should have as its officer a man whom its members do not know, a man who must begin by making their acquaintance?[44]

Paul: In contrast you are proposing that local churches take initiative in selecting those who *already* are serving as leaders?

Roland: Vocation to the ministry of the church has two sides. If it is important that people should be convinced that they are called of God to serve, it is also of importance that the church which they are to serve should be convinced that they are the best people to serve her. The local church must be led by people whom it respects and whose services it will accept.[45]

Paul: Why do you put the call of the church before the internal call to a vocation?

Roland: Nowhere in the Bible do we find that men were invited to offer themselves for the priesthood. In the New Testament we hear nowhere of men being invited to offer themselves for any office in the church.[46]

Paul: Is it not important that a person should feel inwardly called to minister?

Roland: Were the call of the church put first, the internal vocation would respond to that.[47]

Paul: Why not encourage the best young people to put themselves forward?

Roland: Many of the best men would decline to put themselves forward. They know that to fulfill the office they must have the moral support of their congregation, and that it would be fatal to open the door to the jibe that they were putting themselves on a pedestal.[48]

Often those who object to the idea of voluntary clergy are trying to imagine a voluntary cleric in the position of the present stipendiary, and saying that is impossible. That is because they were thinking of one person in sole charge of a parish. The apostles always ordained several clergy for each place. The one-man system, which concentrates all authority in a single individual, is not ideal. No one person concentrates in himself all the various qualities which are necessary for the manifold activities of a church. A few people are singularly gifted, and even they do not do everything with equal efficiency.[49]

Paul: Some fifty years ago you predicted that the supporters of remunerated clergy would spread the services of that one man thinner and thinner. "They urge us," you said, "to supply motorcars in order that one man may cover a wider area than he does now; presently I suppose they will ask for aeroplanes; and in the end urge that the proper way to provide church services for scattered congregations is to install wireless receivers in all the little churches, and then those churchmen who can provide their own installation can stay at home and those who cannot will be able to go to the church to hear hymns sung by professional choristers and sermons preached by professional preachers."[50] Now that this has all happened, what is your real concern?

Roland: No doubt the hearers will be edified and exercise their religious emotions in a highly agreeable manner; but the church of God, the organized society of faithful men, will still be remote from their lives.[51]

Paul: Unlike most church leaders today you are not concerned about shortage of clergy.

Roland: I suggest that the shortage in England is an answer to our prayers, a judgment and a sign pointing us to a larger and fuller conception of the church.[52]

Paul: Roland, you have disturbed us enough for a lifetime! One final question is a personal one. Though you have been a remunerated church worker for many years, you tried to live as nearly as possible the life of a voluntary priest. What is the most important thing you had to learn through the many difficulties you had as a tentmaker?

Roland: That experience has helped me to understand the inwardness of the thing.[53]

9. The Spirituality of a Tentmaker

There is a place for paid ministers and for tent-makers in the church. What is crucial to both is an inward, spiritual matter. In the first century when Paul, the most famous tentmaker, was trained for his ministry, there were paid philosophers and teachers wandering about the Roman world. Paul dissociated himself radically from them. As Gene Thomas has often put it,

We could hardly find a better candidate for the professional ministry than the apostle Paul. He could start a new church in a few weeks. He was undoubtedly the most brilliant theologian of the early church. He could write profound letters (and could have written more than he did if he were supported). He had the ability to teach thousands of hours a year. Our calculation of the Western Text of Acts 19:9 suggests that he taught "from the fifth to the tenth hour." Since Paul taught for two years he must have taught about three thousand hours. Why didn't he make the big sacrifice and go into the ministry? Paul did make the big sacrifice: he stayed *out* of the professional ministry. He gave up his right to be supported by those to whom he had been sent. Now how do we train people to give up rights? That surely is one of the problems of equipping tentmakers. Paul's correspondence and his recorded speech in Acts are sprinkled with comments that instruct us in the spirit and motivation of tentmakers.

Exploring the Heart of a Tentmaker

When advocating self-supported ministry, *Paul,* although he does not specifically say that Jesus the carpenter was his model, *quotes the Lord: "It is more blessed to give than to receive"* (Acts 20:35). Ironically these very words are used today to exhort the congregation to support the church budget (and the supported staff). But these words were first given in the context of exhorting people to give their ministry free of charge. And Paul modeled what he taught. "You yourselves know how you ought to follow our example" (2 Thess 3:7). As Roland Allen said, "The most powerful of all teaching is not direct verbal statement, but habitual attitude and action which takes the truth of the idea upon which it is based for granted."[1]

Though he refused the right for himself, *Paul defended the rights of others to be supported* (1 Cor 9:3-12): From the law (v. 9), from the practice of supporting priests in Israel (v. 13), from the words of the Lord Jesus (v. 14), from secular analogies of rewarded labor (v. 7), by analogy to gratitude for material benefits (how much more, then, for spiritual benefits?—v. 11), and by referring to the example of other supported Christian workers (v. 12). Paul made a thorough defense of the right to support. Yet Paul says his own "reward" is to refuse the right. "What then is my reward? Just this: that in preaching the gospel I may offer it free of charge, and so not make use of my rights in preaching it" (v. 18).

From this we learn that tentmakers need to be generous, trained to give *others* freedom to be supported. And they are to do this not grudgingly but with full biblical authority. Tentmakers must welcome and defend the privileges of the supported worker while giving their own ministry free of charge, without covetousness or envy. Being unsupported, Paul was able to see that ministry was intrinsically rewarding. He believed he had chosen the most rewarding path. He could honestly say that he had never coveted what others had (Acts 20:33).

From the same passage (1 Cor 9) we learn that *Paul supported himself because it was expedient.* He worked "night and day," enduring everything "rather than hinder the gospel of Christ" (1 Cor 9:12). He believed that the gospel would be better advanced by his working, than if he were supported.

A friend of mine teaches marketing at our local university. As part of his sabbatical program he spent six weeks observing how a large advertising agency marketed a new frozen dessert on TV. Behind the scenes no one was interested in the product! The food designers, the celebrity hired to push the product, the children brought in to capture a youthful encounter with the product, all did the same thing. After they had put the food in their mouths for the "take," they spat it out in pails. There would be many more shootings and they didn't like the dessert anyway.

That is, after all, what is expected in the advertising world. The actors don't really like what they promote. It's their job to sell you. And that is what is expected in the religious world: paid to preach. Non-Christians are aware of how much money TV evangelists raise, how preoccupied the church is with numbers, money, new buildings, expansion and success.

For someone to minister as a gift is not only beautiful. It is expedient if we would reach our generation for Christ. Quite possibly, the most expedient thing today to reach our largely pagan country is to have fewer supported ministers and more self-supported ministers.

Paul says there is no sacrifice involved in preaching the gospel. He *must* do it, "for I am compelled to preach. Woe to me if I do not preach the gospel!" (1 Cor 9:16). Since he is entrusted with a commission, he is not acting of his own will (9:17). Where there is no choice there is no sacrifice. Paul has no choice in the matter of *whether* he is to be a minister of the gospel. He has been called and commissioned.

What Paul can choose is *how* he ministers the gospel. It is in the manner of his ministry that Paul chooses to sacrifice. All genuine min-

"Well, we do need volunteers."

istry comes out of sacrifice. Paul's sacrifice is to put himself at a disadvantage for the advantage of the gospel.

To the Thessalonians Paul wrote two shocking things about the extent of his commitment. First, he did not eat anyone's food without paying for it (2 Thess 3:6). This means he refused even normal hospitality given to Christian workers and worked to pay for his room and board. Second, he worked "night and day" in order not to be a burden to anyone (3:8). The tentmaker who would follow Paul's model (3:9) will have to grapple with Paul's example of *sacrificing sleep and ministry time for the work which enabled him not to be dependent.*

Shaping the Heart of a Tentmaker

We may learn how this tentmaker's heart is formed by observing the process of Paul's own training as a tentmaker.

Paul was trained *slowly* and *progressively.* It was at least thirteen years after his conversion that Paul was commissioned by the Antiochene church to be a tentmaking missionary (Acts 13:1). If the great apostle himself, with a splendid background of theological education under Gamaliel and a unique Christ-encounter on the Damascus road, took thirteen years to be equipped, we must forever renounce our dependence on packaged three-year leadership training programs. There are no hydroponic tentmakers. They have to be grown in real soil and grown slowly.

Paul was trained *socially.* The relational dimension of his ministry preparation was fundamental. We forget Barnabas and exalt Paul. But it was Barnabas who twice saved Paul for the work of the ministry (Acts 9:27; 11:25). Paul's relationship with Barnabas was fundamental to his equipment. It was Barnabas who went to Tarsus to recruit this controversial young convert. For a whole year Paul and Barnabas taught a Bible study *together.*

Barnabas was succeeded by Silas, Luke, Aquila and Priscilla. These seminal relationships—witnessed to by the repeated phrase "Paul and his company"—were Paul's tentmaking seminary.

Finally, Paul was trained *through risk.* Sacrificing safety, he deliberately put himself in risky situations for God. Sacrificing his body, he worked and ministered beyond his physical limits. Sacrificing self-indulgence and personal pleasure, he pommeled his body (1 Cor 9:27) against appetites and desires that would, he feared, make him a shipwrecked minister. He chose to rejoice in successful work done by others and to go where Christ was not named, thereby sacrificing personal achievement and personal glory.

This last point fully exposes the inwardness of being a tentmaker. What keeps some people from choosing the tentmaking option is fear of burnout. However, tentmakers seldom experience burnout because they have a natural rhythm in their lives as they move from work to ministry to family. Professional ministers or full-time homemakers are more susceptible to burnout because they tend to invest too many expectations in one commitment. We are called to live beyond ourselves, but we are also called to reckon constantly the cost of living this way. But this call to live sacrificially comes in the context of our whole life, not just one aspect of it.

Work, ministry and family—each of these could be a rewarding full-time job. Yet each is dangerous if it possesses us exclusively and entirely. We are to work with all our heart as to the Lord, as though Jesus were our employer. And we will be more rested at the end of our work-day if we really get involved in work. But we were never meant to live for work.

Family and childrearing can also become a total vocation. But to become engaged totally with our family may not serve to disciple our children in the faith. They need to see us involved in life with joy and generosity. They need to see us involved sacrificially with others.

Ministry could be full-time. But we will have more "rest" in ministry if it is not the only thing we do. The real problem today is not burnout (the presumed reason why many will not be tentmakers) but the fear of really getting involved with people.

In order to sustain a life of multiple callings the tentmaker needs to develop patterns of sabbath rest and personal spiritual disciplines. But in place of the sabbath and practicing the presence of God most people keep a large place for hobbies and leisure. The tentmaking rhythm of work, family and ministry, however, may be a more healthy way. On the surface, balancing multiple demanding callings looks like self-denial— and it is. But in God's economy it is the way of finding ourselves and gaining life.

Liberating the Heart of a Tentmaker

"What I hear you saying is that you are not asking the pastor to become a tentmaker but that the layperson should become more involved?"

"Yes," said Gene Thomas to the seminarian's question, "I am saying that. But I'm saying much more. I'm saying that for tentmakers truly to emerge, the church must be radically changed in both structure and spirit."

Since equipping involves relationships and requires structures that facilitate freedom in ministry, obstacles in church structure must be removed and provision made for liberating the full energy of the equipped tentmaker.

First, *there must be room at the top.* The unremunerated minister must be considered to be as significant as the remunerated. In practice this will not happen as long as the clergy reserve the influential positions of pulpit and chairmanship for themselves. The public ministry of the church *at every level and in every way* must be shared by tentmakers and remunerated leaders.

The administration of the ordinances must not become the exclusive office of the paid clergy. Baptisms and the Eucharist should be conducted by various appointed people, not always by the pastor.

To forestall the pulpit's becoming the "world's greatest amateur hour," one church has two teaching periods. One is thirty minutes and is almost always given by an acknowledged teaching elder. The second period is ten minutes and is always used as a way of discovering gifts. Indeed, almost anyone with the elder's approval and with due preparation may bring an exhortation to the fellowship at that time.

I am not saying that those wishing the "top" position should get it. Jesus says the exact opposite. We should fight for the bottom of the pile, to be a servant. But when others say "come up higher" (Lk 14:10), there must be room at the top or tentmakers will never be anything but second-class clergy.

In those churches that practice public ordination or commendation after the pattern of Acts 13:1-2, nothing less than the ordination of voluntary clergy will faithfully conform to the Word of God.

Second, *there must be visible equality.* Unless tentmakers are *seen* to be of equal importance, we will simply have found a more sophisticated way of allowing the clergy to orchestrate the laity.

One December, as our church faced a bleak financial year end, the elders were considering how to cope with a deficit. Two of the elders were supported; eight were tentmakers. We considered allowing the two supported elders to seek outside employment on a temporary basis and rejected this. An end-of-year deficit was not enough reason for the staff to become tentmakers. The supported elders then considered accepting a reduction in salary since there simply would not be enough cash to meet the December budget.

Graeme, the carpenter-contractor in our group, smiled. "Then we will *all* take a cut in salary this year."

In disbelief I asked him to explain what that would mean. "If our equality means anything," he said, "we cannot ask you to be staff with us unless we share the sacrifice. We will all put in from our own livings whatever is needed to share the shortfall equally." Now that is equality!

Third, *there needs to be mutual appreciation in leadership of the unique contributions of remunerated and unremunerated leaders.* Because the paid staff are preoccupied with the church's life and mission more of their waking hours, they will bring certain insights to the leadership process. Because the tentmakers are more "in the world," they will provide a natural check on excessive programming and will be more sensitive to the issues that the church must address in its ministry.

For example, David, a tentmaking elder, listens to the public teaching in our fellowship with the ear of the people. While not a teaching elder, though "apt to teach" in pastoral settings, he serves the teaching staff by expressing the need for simplicity, clarity and relation to Scripture.

Fourth, *tentmakers need affirmation that a complete nonseminary training for ministry is possible.* Publicly and privately, by modeling and exhortation, we must affirm that those who read the Bible through and through seeking to conform themselves to the way of Christ are being equipped for ministry.

Take Tommy for instance. Tommy grew up in the streets of Detroit. For the sheer fun of it he would cruise the streets looking for someone to beat up. School was a matter of physical survival. He never learned to read. His violence was his identity.

Through the witness of a winsome young Jewish Christian, Tommy found a way to give up his hatred for all people and become a whole person in Christ.

But that is not the end. He was encouraged not to study the Bible or to read commentaries but to read the Bible through and through. He learned to read by reading the Bible and poring over Christian classics. He now exudes the Scriptures and fruitfully declares the whole counsel of God. Probably he knows the Bible better than nine out of ten clergy. And he speaks with greater power than most too.

Fifth, *tentmakers must be included in clerical privileges, and support-*

ed workers must wisely deny themselves a dependence on a clerical support system. Pastors frequently run off to midweek pastors conferences and come back with a fistful of new ideas to try out on their church. Would it not be better for the church to see that tentmakers have equal access to continuing education and enrichment opportunities? Why shouldn't the church fund tentmakers to go to pastors workshops and even to compensate for a day taken off work? And should not the remunerated staff seek their primary fellowship and inspiration from their self-supported peers rather than perpetuating a clerical caste system?

Sixth, *we need a shared spirit of sacrifice.* If the cleric is given too much salary, the weak and mediocre are attracted to the profession for the wrong reasons. It is all too true that some people today go into the ministry because they see it as a secure job with good benefits, a "soft touch." It is not, but it is sometimes perceived as this. The solution is not to impose a starvation wage on supported workers, but for these workers to voluntarily adopt a sacrificial lifestyle. Some measure of poverty is to be embraced for the love of Christ.

And for tentmakers to survive three full-time jobs (work, family and ministry), they must also adopt a sacrificial lifestyle. Tentmakers must live a pruned life and literally find leisure and rest in the rhythm of serving Christ (Mt 11:28). They must be willing to forgo a measure of career achievement and private leisure for the privilege of gaining the prize (Phil 3:14).

Many would like to be tentmakers if they could be wealthy and live a leisurely and cultured lifestyle. But the truth is that a significant ministry in the church and the community can come only by sacrifice.

Part V
Equipping the Equipper

10. The Spiritual Equipment of the Equipper

Only a few years ago the North American church stopped—or almost stopped—sending people overseas to become old-style missionaries (those having a position with the power to control and command). Now we send people overseas to work alongside national leaders and to be their servants. The day has come for this change to occur at home. We must train pastoral staff to work as equipping servants. But this is very threatening to traditional structures and pastoral identity for the following reasons.

By being servants, equippers fear losing their place of leadership through a misperception of the change as a move down rather than up the church organization.

By developing others' gifts, equippers fear they may forfeit the privilege of the full exercise of their own. Supported workers may feel insecure about their status and thus driven to work too hard because they are paid to do what others in the church are doing for free.

By mediating between service and leadership, staff equippers may become the rope in a tug of war between those who want ministers to do the ministry and those who want them to facilitate everyone else's ministry.

By choosing to work in plurality, with multiple agendas, with few predictable structures and with accountability shared by several persons, equippers may be candidates for the dreaded disease of burnout.

This is not merely a matter of time management. It is a spiritual issue. Pastors are called to a deep relationship with God so that they will find their identity not in doing but in being. Having renounced the authority of titles, places, positions of influence and unique roles, they are left with the only authority that really counts: life in God.

There are three pressing needs in spiritual leadership today: *depth, discernment* and *discipline.*

We need depth because, as Richard Foster says, "superficiality is the curse of our age."[1] Evangelical Christianity is, by and large, shallow. It has cultivated either an arid intellectualism or a mindless emotionalism. Christians are educated and active. Many are now effervescently happy. But they are not very deep. We need discernment not only because the Christian worker today is inundated with counterfeit spiritualities but because so much that passes for evangelical Christianity is just the husk of holy things. We need discipline because the most blatant sin of evangelical Christianity is laziness. Believing that Jesus has done it all, evangelicals feel there is nothing they need do, and so become soft and flabby.

Cultivating Depth with God

Knowledge and experience of God is the longing of a whole generation outside the church. It is the hunger at the heart of the spiritual secularism of our day.

Spiritual secularism. It is commonplace to observe that we are now living in a religious, not a secular age. "In 1963," writes Jeff Nuttall, "the mere mention of the God concept was good for a laugh. By 1965 it was many people's most serious concern."[2] In 1959 Martin Marty predicted that the dominant religion in America soon would be "religion in general."[3] In *Soul Friend,* Kenneth Leech has documented the symptoms: the spiritual longings of the youth culture of the 1960s; the search for a spiritual meaning in the drug experience; the exploration of nonchemical consciousness raising through meditation, chanting, fasting, yoga and Eastern religions.[4] This has only intensified in recent years.

This new religiosity demands religious experience. The equipping minister today faces a generation that wants to experience God, not to be told about him. Rational historical apologetics is rarely heard amid the clamor for direct encounter. Who wants to be given "reasons" for faith when you can have a direct experience of the object of faith?

Christianity is uniquely suited to meet this challenge. Christ's invitation to "come and see" (Jn 1:39) and Paul's "in Christ" mysticism witness to the experiential base for Christian discipleship. But are we meeting this challenge?

As part of my equipping ministry I spend three or four weekends each year leading people into the disciplines of the spiritual life. I join them as a fellow novice. The most fruitful discipline we do on such weekends is twenty hours of silence. When we break the fast of speech and share the fruit of silence, we are aware that what we have has truly come from God rather than from another human being. Too much of ministry today is secondhand. We give stale bread to one another because we haven't taken the time to feed on the Bread of Life for ourselves.

Superficial Christianity. Paradoxically, while ours is an age of proliferating religiosity, it is also an age of superficial Christianity. Superficial Christianity does not take us beyond ourselves. By concentrating on experiences of God and gifts from God rather than the person of God, we limit God to our own subjective experiences. The apostles were convinced that God was God whether they experienced him or not. God transcends our experience; he "is greater than our hearts" (1 Jn 3:19).

Christianity is superficial often because it is founded on a wrong diagnosis. Much that passes for Christianity is a disguised attempt to reach God by spirituality, to attain consciousness of God. But Christ speaks not to our consciousness but to our conscience. Luther put it this

*"Congratulations, Reverend! Your program to mobilize the laity was so successful
we don't even need you anymore!"*

way: "To come to the Father is not to ascend with wings to heaven but
with heartfelt confidence to submit oneself to Him as to a Gracious
Father."[5] True spirituality is never far from justification, never far from
the cross, never far from the question, How can I stand before a holy
God?

According to James I. Packer, much current Christianity is a pleasure-
oriented, "Jacuzzi" religion—sensuous, floppy, laid-back, not in any way
demanding. Such a faith offers a warm welcome, a warm choir, a warm,
back-scratching use of words in prayer and preaching and a warm cheer-
ful afterglow. Packer concludes, that if "we embrace a self-absorbed
hedonism of relaxation and happy feelings, while dodging tough tasks,
unpopular stances and exhausting relationships—we should fall short
of biblical God-centeredness and the cross-bearing life to which Jesus
calls us, and advertise to the world nothing better than our own dec-
adence."[6]

Superficial Christianity is relationally superficial, even promiscuous.
We chatter our lives away in numerous shallow relationships and with
God. Few people have soul friends and our greatest loneliness is often
experienced in the church itself. The twelfth-century Cistercian Aelred

of Rievaulx wrote that the quality of our friendships is the measure of our reality with God.[7]

The current Christian context focuses on performance, applauds measurable results and encourages a flurry of activity. But the heart of an equipper is to release *others* into ministry. Often this is neither measurable nor pleasurable.

True spirituality. In the face of spiritual secularism and superficial Christianity, the equipper must discern true spirituality. Jesus defined true spirituality in his little-understood saying, "Your eye is the lamp of the body" (Lk 11:34). Both Matthew and Luke report this word but in significantly different contexts.

In Matthew (6:22-23) Jesus was speaking about having our treasure in heaven. He says we cannot serve two masters: God and money. He warns us that while we may think we are spiritually deep, we may be walking in darkness. So it is essential that our eye be single and sound. But how are we to know whether we have a single eye? I believe that Jesus tells us in Luke's report.

In Luke (11:33-36) the single-eye teaching is sandwiched between Jesus' interaction with the crowd and his interaction with the Pharisees. The crowds wanted signs and experiences as an indication of true spirituality. Jesus would give them no sign but himself, the sign of Jonah. The Pharisees wanted a religion of outward behavior and performance.

Over against the desires of the crowds and the Pharisees, and contradicting our modern materialists who want to praise God and get rich, Jesus called his hearers to simple faith in the Lord, to simplicity and singleness of sight. Jesus called all three groups just to look at him. That is the healthy eye.

In doing so he also told us how we can know whether our eye is healthy. We know we have a single eye not by looking at the eye but by observing the effects of our sight (our spirituality). Jesus said, "When your eyes are good, your whole body also is full of light" (Lk 11:34). "Therefore," he concluded, "if your whole body is full of light, and no part of it dark, it will be completely lighted, as when the light of a lamp shines on you" (11:36).

We have spiritual depth *when our whole life is illuminated.* "No part of it dark" means that absolutely every part of our life is illuminated by Christ. True spirituality is total. It is earthy. It has very little to do with worship services and everything to do with life.

The New Testament is full of this earthy spirituality. There is hardly a verse that associates worshiping God with worship services. Over and over again we are called to worship God in life (Rom 12:1; Jas 1:27; Mt 10:42; Heb 11:11-16; 1 Pet 3:7; Col 3:17).

Often I have the opportunity to share the anguish of young people making vocational decisions today. Many of them feel that there is nothing worth doing in the so-called secular world and they want to "go into the ministry." They are world-weary at eighteen or twenty-two.

When I hear someone say, "I couldn't work for a corporation with a profit motive or which demands more than forty hours a week," I say something like this: "Do you know that the Christian slaves to whom Paul wrote were working sixteen hours a day for masters that were fornicating with the female slaves, making dirty business deals with traders from other parts of the Roman Empire and going to the baths and gymnasium at night for orgies? To these slaves Paul says, 'Treat your masters as though they were Jesus. You are not working for them but for Jesus. And it is worship.' "

True spirituality must go that deep. It must be that earthy. It must make the whole body full of light.

Discerning What Is True

As well as seeing through counterfeit spirituality and superficial Christianity, the equipper must discern what is good and true in the world, in the church and in Christian service.

Discerning worldliness. Sex, money and fame are the obvious hazards to Christian workers. One of the three usually brings them down in shame. And the deadness of these worldly workers reproduces itself in deadness.

But, as Henri Nouwen suggests, there are even more subtle hazards. The equipper cannot afford to be unaware of these. In the temptations of Jesus, Nouwen finds a pattern of testing of our own ministries in relation to the world.

The temptation to turn stones into bread is the temptation to be seemingly relevant. This is the temptation to do something that is needed and can be appreciated by people—to make productivity the basis of our ministry. In yielding our identity to what we produce, we offer *ourselves* as bread to people rather than offering "every word that comes from the mouth of God" (Mt 4:4).[8]

"Throw yourself down" (Mt 4:5), the second temptation which the Spirit of Jesus in us experiences, is the temptation to be spectacular. It is an appeal to be seen and heard. It is sometimes said that the biggest problem of Christian workers is unappreciated greatness. But the problem beneath the problem is a self that is insecure, doubtful and lonely, that lives for the praise of others rather than the praise of God. The worldly minister serves the expectations and approval of others. "Sadly," Nouwen remarks, "this hunger is never satisfied."[9]

The temptation to be powerful is implied in the devil's offer of the whole world if only the minister would bow down and worship Satan. It is, Nouwen suggests, the most seductive of the three temptations. It invites us to accept controlling positions or to use manipulative techniques, even under the pretense of preaching or counseling or administering for God.

These forms of worldliness can be renounced only by undivided attention to God. "Worship the Lord your God, and serve him only" (Mt 4:10) is the call to honor God enough to be powerless and to be downwardly mobile.

Jesus chose, as a fourth alternative, the way of the cross. The cross is the point of intersection between the world and the church. Paul knew this glorious truth when he said that through the cross "the world has been crucified to me, and I to the world" (Gal 6:14). It is the secret of being in the world without being of it. It is the source of the equipper's freedom from the world and therefore the source of freedom to be given to the world as broken bread and poured-out wine.

Discerning the body. In the East African revival of the 1930s the believers were led to ask one another: Are you repenting? Are you walking in the light? Are you being broken? It is this third question which is often hardest for Christian workers because it questions our relationship to the church. How do we really stand with the body of Christ?

Discerning our relationship to the body of Christ is exactly what we must do before we celebrate the Eucharist. "Anyone who eats and drinks without recognizing the body of the Lord eats and drinks judgment on himself" (1 Cor 11:29). Paul further implies that failing to walk in full fellowship with our brothers and sisters could be the real reason why so many are sick and some die prematurely. Discerning the body is the call to love the church as it is. The church is Jesus' funny valentine and he died for love of her. That is the reality against which our pride breaks.

Brokenness, then, is not simply recognizing our psychological or spiritual weakness and allowing ourselves to be vulnerable. Brokenness is not simply keeping short accounts with our brothers and sisters, repenting, confessing and walking in the light. Brokenness is what must happen if we are ever to be unconditionally committed to the church as it is.

F. Kefa Sempangi, who was formed spiritually during the Ugandan revival, put the matter incisively:

> Hardly any of us can go to his own Christian community and say: "This is my body which is broken for you. I am laying all my professional skills, abilities, and economic resources at your disposal. Take them and use them as you see fit." We cannot say this, because we are not broken. We are too proud to give our lives away to people who are not perfect. We don't want to lose ourselves for sinners. We want to find the perfect person and the perfect community, but we never find them. So, like Judas, we make only a partial commitment to the body of believers to which we belong, and we find our identity in our rebellion from them.[10]

When I first read this I wept. I know what it is to be hurt by the church. So I hold back from a full commitment because I do not want to risk being hurt again. I take control of my own ministry and use the church to accomplish my own vocational goals.

My tears came because I realized that it is only now that I can say to my fellowship: "This is my body which is broken for you." But they are tears of joy too for now I truly belong. The church which is the means of crucifying my pride is a means of grace to me. That is the inwardness of equipping the saints in the context of the local church. It is not simply a matter of saying that training happens best in the local church. It is saying that the deepest work of relational equipping cannot happen until we discern what is our actual relationship to the body of Christ. The mystery of the sacrament is that healing comes through brokenness. Wholeness in Christ springs from brokenness in the body.

Discerning the one thing necessary. Applying the gift of discernment to my own relationship to ministry is something I have often been called to do. One Saturday evening I was particularly anxious about my Sunday sermon. Over and over I prayed, "Let me be a faithful servant, please." God broke into my consciousness with this message, "I want you simply to be my son." God was concerned with who I am.

One hazard of the equipping ministry is to make your relationship to God a product of your ministry. This is the idolatry of ministry. Ministers are producers of spirituality but seldom consumers. They pray, study, meditate and reflect because they are equipping others. They are spiritual because their work requires it. But the reverse should be the case. Our relationship with God should give rise to ministry. And gratitude, rather than need, should be the primary motive.

Equippers can also mistake people's needs for the call of God. This too is a ministry idolatry for we allow ourselves to be controlled by needs rather than by God's priorities.

While Jesus was open to being interrupted by a pressing need, he did not allow his ministry to be shaped by the needs that impinged on his life. He was ruled by an inner principle of conformity to the will of the Father. He did not heal all the sick people he saw. He did not address himself to all the social problems of his day. He did not make himself continuously available. He was free to dismiss the crowds (Mk 6:45).

The need is not the call. And nothing will interfere with our devotion to Christ more than our service for him. Busyness is not wrong but the wrong busyness is, especially if it arises from the need to be needed. Our deepest need is not to be needed but to be rooted in God.

There is also the hazard of seeking an immediate reward. Equippers are called to discern that service to God is not *for* anything at all. That was the devil's question about Job: "Does Job fear God for nothing?"

(Job 1:9). Doesn't he have an ulterior motive for being so faithful, so zealous?

Like the merchants and moneychangers in the Temple we may make a percentage on other people's worship. Visible rewards, results, esteem, praise and approval are all currencies in the trade. The judgment of Jesus is poignant and clear: "They have received their reward in full" (Mt 6:16). To demand to see the results of our equipping is to insist on a reward now. We can have our reward now or later—but not both.

So we are called to walk by faith and to serve God, no matter how useless we seem to be. As Oswald Chambers put it: "We have to get rid of this notion 'Am I of any use?' and make up our minds that we are not, and we may be near the truth. It is never a question of being of use, but of being of value to God Himself."[11]

Men have much to learn from the women in our churches in this regard. In the past, by our structures and priorities, the church has communicated to women, "You don't need a place, a role, status or a prestigious public ministry—just serve the Lord." Men need not only to hear what they have said to women but also to observe what women have done. Faithfully, like Mary, they have heeded the call to sit at Jesus' feet and do the one thing necessary (Lk 10:42).

Disciplines of True Spirituality

The most blatant sin of evangelical Christianity is what Bonhoeffer called cheap grace, grace without discipleship—Christianity without spiritual discipline.

The call to recover spiritual discipline has not fallen of late on deaf ears. Richard Roster's excellent book *The Celebration of Discipline* has done much to awaken the hunger of God's people for a deeper spirituality. Instead of asking for more activity or more knowledge or even more skills for ministry, the contemporary Christian is often saying, Teach me to pray. Help me to love God with all my heart and soul. Teach me to meditate on Scripture. Help me to use my imagination in prayer. Train me in the practice of the presence of God. Be my spiritual director.

This genuine request amounts to this challenge: Equipper, equip thyself! For where can they go for spiritual direction? Many Protestants have turned to Catholic sisters and brothers because of the poverty of their own leaders.

Over the last few years I have found that weekend retreats are strategic for the cultivation of spiritual discipline. In the course of forty-eight hours we are able to teach and practice many of the disciplines of the spiritual life and to give some people a fresh start in their pilgrimage. But there is something more important than retreats.

What we need is a philosophy of congregational spiritual formation. People grow up best in a family, not a monastery. The entire life of the local church is the ultimate context for training each person in maturity in Christ. It is in the body that we can best discover the therapeutic and formative disciplines of growing in Christ. Many have found it useful to divide these disciplines into three categories: the upward journey, the inward journey and the outward journey.

The upward journey. Spiritual disciplines are not ways of finding God. Rather they are ways of making ourselves available to the seeking Father (Jn 4:23; Lk 15:20). Blaise Pascal once said, "Thou wouldst not be seeking Him if thou hadst not already found Him." The Christian starting point in the upward journey is where classic spirituality ends, as Richard Lovelace demonstrates in *Dynamics of Spiritual Life.* Classical mysticism moves through three stages: the cleansing of one's life, illumination and union with God. Christian spirituality reverses the order. It starts with union with God through Jesus, the gracious gift of justification and the Spirit sent into our hearts. Then, as a result, we move through illumination by the Holy Spirit to a consequent cleansing through the process of sanctification. Lovelace remarks, "True spirituality is not a superhuman religiosity; it is simply true humanity released from bondage to sin and renewed by the Holy Spirit."[12]

It is nevertheless a great work to make ourselves truly available to God. Is there a greater work? To do it we must build patterns of solitude into our lives. Russell Baker once said that "the number of places where a person can escape entertainment get fewer every year."[13] Sadly, the church is not exempt. But if we are to become deep and discerning people, we will have to restore the right to brood undisturbed.

The disciplines of the upward journey—thanksgiving, praise and adoration, confession, keeping short account with God—are rich, as both Scripture and Christian tradition witness.

Bible meditation—which is more than just intellectual study—means savoring the Word, chewing it over and over again. I once meditated profitably for several months on "Your sins have been forgiven on account of his name" (1 Jn 2:12). The development of a sanctified imagination is part of the upward journey. We are to use our God-given capacity to create images. And we must learn waiting in prayer, listening in solitude, sometimes waiting for him for long hours.

I once waited in a restaurant for an hour to meet an old friend. He never came. Later I found that he had spent the same hour waiting for me just a few yards away in another restaurant with a similar name. Sometimes on the upward journey we feel that way. But there is no wrong place to wait for the Father. Even the desire to know him better is a witness that he has preceded us in every step toward him. He is waiting for us to wait. He is at the same table in the same house.

The inward journey. The Psalms witness to the importance of this aspect of spiritual formation. Take Psalm 42:5 for instance:

Why are you downcast, O my soul?
Why so disturbed within me?
Put your hope in God,
for I will yet praise him,
my Savior and my God.

The psalmist is quite frankly *talking to himself* in the Lord's presence! Though some spiritual directors start with the inward journey, the scriptural order is to start with God and then to proceed to ourselves. In the sixteenth century St. Theresa of Avila said, "As I see it we shall never succeed in knowing ourselves unless we seek to know God."[14] The prodigal "came to himself" (Lk 15:17) because he knew what kind of father he could come to. With our Father we can risk being real.

This kind of inward journey is far more productive work than simple navel-gazing or overscrupulous confession. A certain priest who heard the confession of a nun said it was "like being stoned to death with popcorn"! Nor is the inward work simply the natural high of exploring "the private Sea, the Atlantic and Pacific Ocean of one's being alone,"[15] as Thoreau did at Walden Pond. It is not self-realization or self-actualization. It is the reality of being found by the Father just as we are.

For this inward journey we have many available disciplines: the discipline of keeping a journal (of which Ps 42:5 is an example); the discipline of walking through our lives with Jesus—retracing our personal history in his presence; I have often encouraged such a journey on extended retreats or a day of complete silence. We have also the discipline of inner healing by which we can be released from painful memories.[16]

I once attended a pastors conference during which, in a prayer time, a prophecy was given to a brother who was flirting with burnout. It came purportedly from the Lord and was delivered in sepulchral tones: "Be not discouraged or cast down, my child. Never mind. I get that way myself sometimes." We laughed uproariously.

I report this partly to demythologize burnout, a phenomenon that has become faddish and which keeps many people from really getting involved in ministry. My report of this somewhat questionable prophecy is that humor is an act of worship. It is a recognition of our creatureliness. It is an admission that we had better not take ourselves too seriously. Perhaps it was a true prophecy after all since it is where the inward journey should take us—back to being creatures.

The outward journey. If our spiritual disciplines do not lead us to have a burning passion for some aspect of society or for suffering people, it is heresy. My wife, Gail, and I are burdened about what is happening to marriages in our society. For others the upward and inward journeys lead to a concern for social justice, disarmament, abortion or poverty.

Religion, contrary to what the philosopher Alfred North Whitehead said, is not "what the individual does with his solitariness."[17] Rather it is what we do with Jesus and our brother. And it is also allowing ourselves to be converted to a right relationship to the world.

The disciplines of the outward journey are intended to lead us into practical love and sacrificial service in the world. Intercessory prayer is but one of the steps. Repentance and confession are crucial to our engagement with others. We cannot pray the Lord's Prayer without it: "forgive us our trespasses as we forgive those who trespass against us." As Elizabeth O'Connor points out, "St. Augustine called this the terrible petition, and terrible it is, because it states with alarming clarity that what we so desperately need for ourselves is conditioned upon our extending it to others."[18]

Can we pray for those hardest to love? Those who have hurt us and rejected us?

O'Connor speaks of this engagement with others through solitude as the important work of releasing people from wrongs done to us. She says, "I am free only when I become responsible for who I am and what I become. My forgiveness is my willingness to be held accountable for my own life. My revolutionary vocation is to lay myself open to being hurt by even those who have hurt me once before."[19]

How can equippers get the time for these three disciplines? They must steal it, steal it from work, from play, from sleep. A seasoned worker I know rises at five and uses drugs to get going—tea! He also has been know to wear Walkman earphones with the earphone plug slipped into his back pocket unattached! People think he is listening to Bach when he is actually talking with the Lord. Others, like me, need a day away every two weeks, completely alone. An elder I know goes window shopping every Friday night in a large mall and finds solitude in the midst of the mob. (Every person to his own form of insanity!)

Indeed we should not be afraid to be crazy for God. That's what the single eye is all about. We can worship while driving our car, going to the bathroom, doing the dishes or mowing the lawn. For equippers this is not simply a preference. It is a matter of survival. They cannot afford to be away from the Father's presence. They must constantly find their identity not in what they do but in whose they are. For the goal of the Christian life, even more than its beginning, is simply to be a child in the Father's presence—to cry "Abba, Father"—and to do this in all of our life. That is reality in the spiritual life. And it is how the equipper needs to be equipped.

11. One Truly Liberated Layperson

Joseph Hovsepian is a lay pastor, a tent-maker-elder and businessman in Montreal, Quebec. *(My job is too demanding to allow me to engage in serious Christian leadership.)* Joseph owns and runs a small electronic equipment retail store which requires much more than forty hours a week. *(I can't make my business life a ministry without sacrificing efficiency.)* Joseph says that his store is his pulpit. *(I couldn't survive without separating home from work and work from ministry.)* Joseph lives over his store and walks to his church, Temple Baptist. *(He must be single.)* Joseph is married and his wife, Jessie, not only shares his ministry and storekeeping but has a ministry of her own through music and hospitality. *(Surely they have no children at home.)* Joseph and Jessie have two children, both teen-agers. Their parents live nearby and require help. They are not independently wealthy but came to this country penniless. Their native languages are

Greek and Armenian, not English.

Their ministry is not limited to only one local church; Joseph chairs an interchurch ethnic fellowship that brings together people from more than thirty ethnic churches for fellowship and mutual enrichment. Recently, he added to his many responsibilities being chairman of a major crusade to the ethnic populations of Montreal.

When, from time to time, Joseph's home church is without a pastor, he functions as the lay pastor, visiting the sick, coordinating services, giving leadership, working with the group ministry (the elders) and preaching. Even when there is a remunerated pastor, Joseph continues to give leadership as a coordinator and pastoral servant. He exemplifies *the importance of keeping a place at the top for the tentmaker.* He is an example of a truly liberated layperson.

Joseph's mature leadership did not just happen. And it has not come about overnight. It is now twenty-five years since he arrived in Halifax as an Armenian immigrant from Athens, not knowing a word of English. He was a new Christian. His godly parents, who at that time were still in Greece, prayed for him daily and wrote letters with appropriate scriptural promises. Now at forty-four Joseph is a mature leader. Joseph matured gradually; *maturity takes time.*

Apart from a technical course in electronics, Joseph has very little formal education beyond high school. But he is "apt to teach" and able to use the Scriptures in pastoral situations—to win to Christ, to confound error and to exhort brothers and sisters. Joseph would have appreciated going to Bible school or taking courses to prepare for the ministry, but this was not practical. Consequently, *his education* for the ministry *took place within the ongoing life of the local church.* He read the Bible on his own over and over again, loving the Word.

Significantly, the moment of greatest scriptural growth for him, by his own confession, was a period of doctrinal strife within the church. Rather than relying exclusively on the advice of outside professionals, Joseph and Jessie set out to discover for themselves what Scripture said and not merely by a cursory examination. They spent hours each day in Bible study and prayer until they were sure what they believed and why. A problem became an opportunity for growth.

Another factor in the maturation of this tentmaking couple has been their *stability*. Joseph and Jessie have remained in the same church and in the same neighborhood for twenty-four years. Theirs was not an ideal church. By normal ecclesiastical standards it was not even a "successful" church. Many times it was suggested to them that a more fruitful arena of service could be found than this multicultural inner-city church of one hundred members.

At one strategic point Joseph was the youth leader for a large Armenian evangelical group that met in the church building. The group became a church and moved out. Joseph stayed, even though his heart and burden was to start an evangelical work among the Armenian people. "This is my church," he says. "It was the church to which God led me when I came to this city as an immigrant. It was the people of this church who taught me to speak English. I was baptized, married here and my children have been baptized here. Temple Baptist Church is my church, our church."

By staying in one place for twenty-four years, Joseph created an equipping situation for himself without realizing it. He grew by working through the problems of the church rather than running to another seemingly problem-free situation. He learned to deal with his own weaknesses too as he interacted with the same family in Christ over many years.

Joseph had *many models of ministry*. First and foremost, his parents taught him, by their example in Greece, to serve the Lord in the church wholeheartedly. They gave their time freely to practical tasks—cleaning the building, taking strangers into their home and being servants for Christ's sake. His parents lived for the kingdom of God, spoke the Word of God to him from his youth and prayed for him every day. Joseph's mother, though handicapped with an artificial leg, modeled sacrificial service and faithful involvement in the local church. There was no greater treasure which his parents desired than that each of their children should be in Christ. Though made poor in this world through the Armenian massacre of 1917, they have indeed become rich in eternity.

Joseph says that from his first pastors (me and my wife) he learned how to care for people in Christ, how to nurture people, how to open up his home and use it for ministry. Even nontentmakers can model ministry to aspiring tentmakers!

A third model was an evangelist, also a supported Christian worker. This evangelist believed that Joseph had capacities for evangelism. Like Joseph's father, this evangelist tried to persuade Joseph to go "into the ministry"; he needed and should have a pulpit. But the exhortation was not wasted, as Joseph was gently discipled into making his store into a pulpit, a place where the good news of Jesus could be shared in the marketplace.

From three models Joseph learned to serve, to shepherd and to share his faith. It takes more than one model. None of us is an adequate model alone. Together, as the body of Christ, we are.

Further, Joseph was given *opportunities to experience ministry.* Learning to be a minister was a matter of trial and error. He was catapulted into leadership with the Armenian youth group that met in his home church. That gave him room to try leading, speaking, administering and leading a prayer meeting. When that group left to start an autonomous church, Joseph threw in his lot with his home church as they tried to restructure their life around five ethnic congregations (English, Spanish, Italian, Armenian and Greek), meeting as part of one Canadian church. Since the Sunday morning teaching was in English, Joseph was asked to translate for the Greek and Armenian believers. He learned to preach using my sermon notes! When I left that church Joseph was needed as an interim lay pastor. Over the years, five churches were born out of Temple Baptist. Each moment of birth called for leadership both in the new work and in the mother church.

But the final and full credit for Joseph's history must go to the Great Shepherd. Most of Joseph's motivation for ministry came directly from the Lord. He had a burden to reach the lost. That can be developed by training but never created by it. He had a burden to reach his own Armenian people. That burden went beyond an ethnic loneliness to a profound concern to reach a generation of immigrants. Early in his days in Montreal that burden led him to track down one other evangelical Armenian serving as a Sunday-school teacher and to pray with that brother that God might use them to start an Armenian congregation. They were used to help with two!

More recently God gave Joseph the burden for unity among all the ethnic churches in Montreal. Joseph longed for a new cross-cultural Pentecost to replace the current ecclesiastical Babel. So, as a layperson, he called together all the pastors of ethnic churches in the city for prayer. This has resulted in a large monthly gathering of believers from over thirty churches, each believer bringing a prayer, a word, a tongue, a revelation, a song in his or her own language.

What makes ministers? Essentially and ultimately it is the Lord who makes them. And the method is only partly known to us. "As you do not know the path of the wind, or how the body is formed in a mother's womb, so you cannot understand the work of God, the Maker of all things" (Eccles 11:5). He is the physician reducing the fracture, the fisherman mending the net, the stonemason rebuilding the wall, the potter shaping the clay, the model parent and the one who fits all the pieces together without forcing them. He is more concerned than we are to thaw out his own frozen assets, to liberate his own people, his laity.

That it is the Lord who makes ministers is a great relief to us—and fresh incentive to join him in the task of equipping.

Notes

Preface
[1]Elton Trueblood, *The Incendiary Fellowship* (New York: Harper and Row, 1967), p. 41.

Chapter 1: The Confessions of a Late-Starting Layperson
[1]This is the reading in KJV, RV, ASV and RSV (1952 ed.).
[2]Marjorie Warkentin, *Ordination: A Biblical-Historical View* (Grand Rapids: Eerdmans, 1982), p. 187.
[3]Some Scriptures to study concerning financial support and self-support are: Acts 20:13-38; 1 Cor 9:11-12; 1 Thess 2:9; 4:11; 2 Thess 3:8-10; 1 Tim 5:17-18.
[4]Hendrik Kraemer, *A Theology of the Laity* (London: Lutterworth Press, 1958), pp. 51-52.
[5]Mark Gibbs and T. Ralph Morton, *God's Frozen People* (London: Fontana Books, 1964), p. 20.
[6]George Hunston Williams, "The Ancient Church," in *The Layman in Christian History*, ed. Stephen Charles Neill and Hans-Ruedi Weber (London: SCM Press,

1963), p. 52.
[7]W. E. Vine, *Expository Dictionary of New Testament Words,* 4 vols. (London: Oliphants, 1940), 3:175.
[8]Gibbs and Morton, *God's Frozen People,* p. 158.
[9]Abbé Michonneau, *Revolution in a City Parish* (Westminster, Md.: Newman Press, 1965), pp. 131-32.

Chapter 2: The Abolition of the Laity: Biblical Foundations

[1]Markus Barth, *Ephesians, Translation and Commentary on Chapters 4—6,* vol. 34A, The Anchor Bible (Garden City, N.Y.: Doubleday, 1981), p. 479.
[2]Lawrence Richards and Clyde Hoeldtke, *Theology of Church Leadership* (Grand Rapids: Zondervan, 1980), p. 189.
[3]Richard Halverson, *How I Changed My Thinking about the Church* (Grand Rapids: Zondervan, 1972), pp. 73-74.
[4]Barth, *Ephesians,* p. 449.
[5]Stephen Clark, *Building Christian Communities* (Notre Dame, Ind.: Ave Maria Press, 1972).
[6]Ibid., p. 38.
[7]Richard Pollay, "The Distorted Mirror: Reflections on the Unintended Consequences of Advertising," Working Paper No. 1005, History of Advertising Archives, University of British Columbia, p. 4.
[8]Frank R. Tillapaugh, *The Church Unleashed: Getting God's People Out Where the Needs Are* (Ventura, Calif.: Regal, 1982), p. 76.
[9]William F. Arndt and F. Wilbur Gingrich, eds., *A Greek-English Lexicon of the New Testament and Other Early Christian Literature* (Chicago: University of Chicago Press, 1957), p. 419.
[10]F. F. Bruce, *The Epistle to the Ephesians* (London: Pickering and Inglis, 1961), p. 86.
[11]Ibid.
[12]Barth, *Ephesians,* p. 450.
[13]Arnold Bittlinger, *Gifts and Graces,* trans. Herbert Klassen (Grand Rapids: Eerdmans, 1967), p. 68.
[14]See George Mallone, "Thus Says the Lord: Prophecy and Discernment," in George Mallone et al., *Those Controversial Gifts* (Downers Grove, Ill.: Inter-Varsity Press, 1983), pp. 31-50.
[15]Oswald Chambers, *My Utmost for His Highest* (New York: Dodd, Mead and Co., 1956), p. 291.

Chapter 3: A Most Unruly and Chaotic Little Bible School

[1]Gibbs and Morton, *God's Frozen People,* pp. 29-30.
[2]Quoted in Paul Benjamin, *The Equipping Ministry* (Cincinnati: Standard Pub-

lishing, 1978), p. 84.
[3]Peter H. Davids and J. Andrew Kirk, "Why Theological Education By Extension?" (Unpublished paper; Vancouver, B.C.: Regent College, 1983), p. 1.
[4]Ibid.
[5]John N. Vaughan, "Schools of Experience," *Christianity Today,* 20 Dec. 1974, p. 17.
[6]Quoted in Richard J. Foster, "A Life of Broad Strokes and Brilliant Hues," *Christianity Today,* 23 May 1980, p. 20.
[7]Trueblood, *Incendiary Fellowship,* p. 45.
[8]V. S. T. Tyndale, "Theological Education: A Global Perspective," (Unpublished paper; Toronto, 1983), p. 21.
[9]Ibid., p. 20.
[10]Quoted in ibid., p. 21.
[11]Ibid., p. 24.
[12]Ibid., p. 30.
[13]Quoted in ibid., p. 14.
[14]Quoted in Tom Allen, *The Face of My Parish* (London: SCM Press, 1958), p. 77.
[15]Michael Green, *Evangelism in the Early Church* (London: Hodder and Stoughton, 1970), p. 205.
[16]Quoted in ibid., p. 206.
[17]Quoted in Elizabeth O'Connor, *Journey Inward, Journey Outward* (New York: Harper and Row, 1968), p. 103.
[18]Johannes Jörgensen, *Saint Francis of Assisi,* trans. T. O'Connor Sloane (Garden City, N.Y.: Doubleday, 1955), p. 5.
[19]Howard Snyder, *The Radical Wesley* (Downers Grove, Ill.: InterVarsity Press, 1980), p. 163.

Chapter 4: How to Build a Church around a Bus Stop

[1]Howard A. Snyder, *The Problem of Wineskins* (Downers Grove, Ill.: InterVarsity Press, 1976), p. 13.
[2]Reproduced from George Mallone, "Developing an Eager Church," *Channels* 1, no. 1 (Fall 1983): 13.
[3]R. Paul Stevens, "Honing the Two-Edged Sword," *Leadership 100,* Nov.-Dec. 1983, pp. 12-15.
[4]Mallone, "Developing an Eager Church," p. 14.
[5]Quoted in Allen, *The Face of My Parish,* p. 82.
[6]Quoted in Tom Allen, *The Agent of Mission: The Lay Group in Evangelism* (Glasgow: Tell Scotland Press, n.d.), p. 11.
[7]Quoted in F. Roy Coad, *A History of the Brethren Movement* (Exeter, Eng.: The Paternoster Press, 1968), p. 269.

[8]George Mallone, *Furnace of Renewal* (Downers Grove, Ill.: InterVarsity Press, 1981), pp. 96-106.
[9]Quoted in John Yoder, "Martin Luther's Forgotten Vision," *The Other Side,* April 1977, pp. 66-67.

Chapter 5: The Ministry of Work
[1]This test is fully described in Ralph Mattson, *Finding a Job You Can Love* (Nashville: Nelson, 1982).
[2]Quoted in Gary R. Collins, *Christian Counseling* (Waco, Tex.: Word Books, 1980), p. 241.
[3]Roland Allen, *The Case for the Voluntary Clergy* (London: Eyre and Spottiswoode, 1930).
[4]Quoted in Roland H. Bainton, *Here I Stand: A Life of Martin Luther* (New York: Mentor Books, 1950), p. 156.
[5]William E. Diehl, *Thank God, It's Monday!* (Philadelphia: Fortress Press, 1982), pp. 190-91.
[6]Quoted in James Houston, "The Theology of Work," in *Professional Priorities—A Christian Perspective* (Christian Medical Dental Society of Canada, 1981), p. 46.
[7]Ibid.
[8]Robert A. Markus, "Work and Worker in Early Christianity," in *Work: Christian Thought and Practice,* ed. John Todd (London: Darton, Longman and Todd, 1960), p. 23.
[9]Daniel Yankelovitch, "New Rules In American Life: Searching for Self-Fulfillment in a World Turned Upside Down," *Psychology Today,* April 1981, p. 76.
[10]Diehl, *Thank God, It's Monday!* p. 171.
[11]Ibid., p. 188.

Chapter 6: Equipping for Mission: Where in the World Are You?
[1]Dietrich Bonhoeffer in a letter from Tegel prison, 1944, quoted in Melanie Morrison, "As One Who Stands Convicted," *Sojourners,* May 1979, p. 15.
[2]Quoted by Origen, "Contra Celsius," in Williams, "Ancient Church," p. 52.
[3]Wilbur Sutherland, "Considerations Affecting a Biblical Theology of the World and Its Implications for the Work of IVCF," unpublished speech, 4 January 1967, p. 4.
[4]Williams, "Ancient Church," p. 46.
[5]Quoted in Elizabeth O'Connor, *The New Community* (New York: Harper and Row, 1976), p. 101.
[6]See Michael Green, *Evangelism in the Early Church.*
[7]Gordon Cosby, *Handbook for Mission Groups* (Waco, Tex.: Word Books, 1975).

[8]Harvey Cox, *The Secular City* (New York: Macmillan, 1965).

[9]E. H. Oliver, *The Social Achievements of the Christian Church* (United Church of Canada, 1930), p. 31.

[10]Williams, "Ancient Church," p. 48.

[11]Oliver, *Social Achievements,* p. 73.

[12]Ibid., p. 101.

[13]John Wesley Bready quoted in Findley Edge, *The Greening of the Church* (Waco, Tex.: Word Books, 1971), p. 97.

[14]Ibid., p. 99.

[15]Ibid., p. 89.

[16]Oliver, *Social Achievements,* p. 116.

[17]Quoted in Elton Trueblood, *The Company of the Committed* (New York: Harper and Row, 1961), p. 101.

[18]Markus Barth, *The Broken Wall: A Study of the Epistle to the Ephesians* (Chicago: Judson Press, 1959), p. 45.

[19]P. T. Forsyth, *The Church and the Sacraments* (London: Independent Press, 1917), p. 29.

Chapter 7: Six Ways to Beat the Solo Ministry Trap

[1]Dr. Seuss, *Yertle the Turtle and Other Stories* (New York: Random House, 1958).

[2]Miriam Adeney, "Women of Fire: A Response to Waltke, Nolland and Gasque," *Crux* 19, no. 3 (Sept. 1983): 31.

[3]Arndt and Gingrich, *Greek-English Lexicon,* p. 418.

[4]Ibid.

[5]Quoted in Michael Griffiths, "Maturity," in *Where Do We Go from Here?* ed. Alan Bamford (Worthing, Eng.: H. E. Walter, 1979), p. 77.

[6]Arndt and Gingrich, *Greek-English Lexicon,* p. 418.

[7]R. Schippers, *"artios,"* in *The New International Dictionary of New Testament Theology,* ed. Colin Brown, 3 vols. (Grand Rapids: Zondervan, 1978), 3:349-50.

[8]Arndt and Gingrich, *Greek-English Lexicon,* p. 120.

[9]Ibid., p. 418.

[10]Stevens, "Honing the Two-Edged Sword," pp. 12-15.

[11]These presentations are substantially reproduced and enlarged in *Crux* 19, no. 3 (Sept. 1983).

[12]James Hurley, *Man and Woman in Biblical Perspective* (Grand Rapids: Zondervan, 1981), p. 176.

[13]Arndt and Gingrich, *Greek-English Lexicon,* p. 419.

[14]Peter Richardson, "Paul Today: Jews, Slaves and Women," *Crux* 18, no. 1 (1981): 35.

[15]John Le Carré, *Smiley's People* (London: Pan Books, 1980), p. 138.
[16]"A Biblical Style of Leadership," *Leadership* (Spring Quarter, 1981): 78.

Chapter 8: The Case for the Voluntary Clergy

[1]Allen, *The Case for Voluntary Clergy.*
[2]Allen himself told his son that his writings would not come into their own until about 1960; Lesslie Newbigin's foreword to Roland Allen, *Missionary Methods: St. Paul's or Ours?* (Grand Rapids: Eerdmans, 1962), p. i.
[3]Ibid., p. ii; Roland Allen's responses in this interview are direct quotations from his writings with only slight editorial changes made for ease of reading.
[4]Ibid., p. 5.
[5]Allen, *Case for Voluntary Clergy,* p. 25.
[6]Ibid., p. 23.
[7]Ibid., p. 26.
[8]Ibid., p. 24.
[9]Ibid., pp. 86-88.
[10]Ibid., p. 80.
[11]Ibid., p. 23.
[12]Ibid.
[13]Ibid., p. 26.
[14]Ibid., p. 40.
[15]Ibid., p. 41.
[16]Ibid., p. 37.
[17]Ibid., p. 51.
[18]Ibid., p. 43.
[19]Ibid., p. 47.
[20]Ibid., pp. 42-43.
[21]Ibid., p. 101.
[22]Ibid., pp. 47, 49.
[23]Ibid., p. 50.
[24]Ibid., p. 81.
[25]Ibid.
[26]Allen, *Missionary Methods,* pp. 160-61.
[27]Allen, *Case for Voluntary Clergy,* p. 82.
[28]Ibid., p. 83.
[29]Ibid., p. 51.
[30]Ibid., p. 297.
[31]Ibid., p. 298.
[32]Ibid., pp. 298-99.
[33]Ibid., p. 298; emphasis added.
[34]Ibid.

³⁵Ibid., p. 300.
³⁶Ibid., p. 303, quoting a Dr. Bright.
³⁷Ibid., p. 300.
³⁸Ibid., pp. 300-301.
³⁹Ibid., p. 57.
⁴⁰Ibid., p. 71.
⁴¹Ibid., p. 74.
⁴²Ibid., p. 54.
⁴³Allen, Missionary Methods, p. 100.
⁴⁴Allen, Case for Voluntary Clergy, p. 263.
⁴⁵Ibid., p. 60.
⁴⁶Ibid., p. 59.
⁴⁷Ibid., p. 61.
⁴⁸Ibid., pp. 60-61.
⁴⁹Ibid., pp. 95-96.
⁵⁰Ibid., pp. 150-51.
⁵¹Ibid., p. 151.
⁵²Ibid., p. 261.
⁵³Ibid., p. 8.

Chapter 9: The Spirituality of a Tentmaker

¹Allen, Case for Voluntary Clergy, p. 128.

Chapter 10: The Spiritual Equipment of the Equipper

¹Richard Foster, Celebration of Discipline (New York: Harper and Row, 1978), p. 1.
²Quoted in Kenneth Leech, Soul Friend (London: Sheldon Press, 1977), p. 5.
³Martin Marty, The New Shape of American Religion (New York: Harper and Row, 1959), pp. 31-44.
⁴Leech, Soul Friend, pp. 5-29.
⁵Quoted in Donald Bloesch, The Crisis of Piety (Grand Rapids: Eerdmans, 1968), p. 109.
⁶James I. Packer, "A View from a Jacuzzi," Regent College Bulletin 11, no. 4 (Fall-Winter 1981).
⁷Aelred of Rievaulx, Spiritual Friendship (Kalamazoo, Mich.: Cistercian Publications, 1977).
⁸Henri Nouwen, "Temptation," Sojourners, July 1981, p. 25.
⁹Ibid., p. 26.
¹⁰F. Kefa Sempangi, "Walking in the Light," Sojourners, February 1978, p. 27.
¹¹Chambers, My Utmost for His Highest, p. 52.
¹²Richard Lovelace, Dynamics of Spiritual Life (Downers Grove, Ill.: InterVarsity

Press, 1979), p. 19.
[13]Quoted in Robert Raines, *Creative Brooding* (New York: Macmillan, 1966), p. 11.
[14]Quoted in O'Connor, *Journey Inward, Journey Outward*, p. 17.
[15]Quoted in William Braden, *The Private Sea: LSD and the Search for God* (Toronto: Bantam Books, 1968), p. 68.
[16]See Rita Bennett, *You Can Be Emotionally Free* (Old Tappan, N.J.: Fleming H. Revell, 1982).
[17]Quoted in Bloesch, *Crisis of Piety*, p. 102.
[18]Quoted in O'Connor, *The New Community*, p. 110.
[19]Ibid., p. 112.